THE MINERS' TRIUMPH

The First English World Cup Win in Football History

2nd Edition

———————

Martin Connolly

First published in Great Britain in 2014 by
Oakleaf Publishing

This second edition published 2018
Copyright © Martin Connolly, 2014, 2018

ISBN 9781718085824

The right of Martin Connolly to be identified as Author of this work has been asserted by him in accordance with the Copyright, Designs and Patents Act 1988.

A CIP catalogue record for this book is available from the British Library. All rights reserved. No part of this book may be reproduced or transmitted in any form or by any means, electronic or mechanical including photocopying, recording or by any information storage and retrieval system, without permission from the Author in writing.
e-mail: oakleafpublisshing@btinternet.com

FRONT COVER IMAGES

The commemorative statue on West Auckland Green.

A post card from Turin sent on winning the Trophy for the second time.

Sir Alex Ferguson and Ed Waugh, co-author of *Alf Ramsey Knew My Grandfather*, a play about the West Auckland football team's world cup win, with the trophy.

Dave Thomas, grandson of 'Ticer' Thomas, who played for England and QPR among others.

THE MINERS' TRIUMPH

This book is dedicated to the memory of the men of West Auckland Football Club who in 1909 and 1911, performed heroically to bring home the Sir Thomas Lipton Trophy.
1909
Jimmy Dickinson, Robert Gill, Jack Greenwell, Captain Bob Jones (Ovington), Thomas Gill, Charlie Parker Hogg, Ben Whittingham, Douglas Crawford, Bob Guthrie, Alf Gubbins, Jock Jones, David 'Ticer' Thomas, Frank 'Tucker' Gill
1911
John Warwick, Tommy Wilson, Fred Dunn, Tommy Riley (Bayles), Charlie Parker Hogg, Robert Guthrie, Bob Jones, Joe Rewcastle, Andy Appleby, Bob Moore, Michael Alderson (Captain), Charlie Cassidy, James Robinson, (Albert Gill, George Summerson Parker and Willie Holmes)
The officials
Syd Barron, Bob Chamberlain, Eddie Meek, Willie Nolli and Robert Hodgson

Martin Connolly

FOREWORD

When I think of the miners who played in the 1909 Tournament in Turin, I find it incredible. How a group of miners, many who had never travelled very far, made a journey by train and boat all that way, is amazing. In this day and age, we take travel for granted but for these men, not much money or possessions, to make that trip was unique. A football team travelling today have great luxury and various coaches and physiotherapists to help. These men, in the clothes they stood up in, did it on their own. They deserve great credit. My granddad was one of these men. I have great memories of him. He spent many hours with me on the field behind our house. In my football career I could use either foot. This was down to my Granddad. He would make me play the ball with both feet. If I complained of being tired as a young five to seven-year-old, he would stretch me to make me use both feet. He was determined that I would become an all-round footballer. This dedication to being a better footballer, I believe was in these miners who went to Italy and inspired them to their victory. A treasured memory I have, is that when I played for St Helen Junior's at the age of seven, the rest of the team were around eleven, we regularly won the league and cup. It was at Shildon we were presented with our winner's medal and my Granddad was asked to present the medals. To have this man, who had won a World Trophy medal, present me with my medal was both emotional and an encouragement. It was fantastic. He was a great granddad and I remember him telling my Dad that I would one day play for England. He was an amazing man and a great role model to me. I would hope that many would be inspired by this great football story, especially young people. I hope that they would see the desire and commitment of these miners who won the Sir Thomas Lipton Trophy. In the modern game there is a lot about money - their achievement was not about the money, it was about skill, courage and a can-do attitude. Their part in the 1909 Tournament cost them financially but they had a love of football in their heart and a desire to be the best and that brought them victory. It is nice to earn a decent living from football, but I would hope that young people will take hold of this story of a bunch of miners, like my Granddad, and be encouraged by what they achieved and to go and play their football with skill and passion. Anything on top of that is a bonus.

David (Ticer) Thomas

INTRODUCTION

'Don't be daft lad!'
In a discussion about football and reflecting on the national side, I had just brought up the great success of England winning the 1966 World Cup with old Jeff, who was posting a parcel at my Post Office in West Auckland. Jeff was a retired miner. His face showed the creases of his years toiling underground. He was proud of his mining background and had often told me tales of the many hardships they endured in the earlier days. Sometimes the heat underground was so extreme, that they worked in their underwear or even naked to carry out the back-breaking task of a hewer. Some men had permanent scars that stood like a dotted line down their back, caused as the scraped along low rooves. These men were tough and indeed brave, as they brought out the fuel that powered industry and advanced the Industrial Revolution. Indeed, the First World War and the necessary production to support it, had the miners at its heart as

without their efforts the tools necessary to get the job done could not have been produced.

'Nae lad - I'll admit it was a great win. Aye beating the Germans was grand. But you know there is another tale to tell about English football. When and which team had the first English World Cup win?'

Old Jeff took in a full chest of air. There was a glint in his eye and the trace of a smirk on his lips. What was he up to, asking an obvious football question? I had just taken up residence in West Auckland a few months before. Sometimes I was never quite sure when he was spinning a yarn or telling the truth. Jeff was a character always up for a bit of leg-pulling.

'Uruguay, they beat Argentina four to one in the first World Cup final. England did not take part. It was held in Uruguay and 1966 at Wembley England won it for the first time, as I have already said.'

That should impress him, I thought. He began to chuckle.

'Nae. Ye have got that wrong. Here I was thinking ye were a canny lad too.'

I tried to open my mouth to argue, but he continued.

'West Auckland, that's the right answer. They were the first English team to win a World Cup.'

This small village, no more than a couple of streets with a few pubs and not much else, was an unlikely place for World Cup winners. Here we go; it was another leg-pull from Jeff.

'Aye Jeff and I am the king of England!'

'I'll say nowt your majesty. Ye go and check it out lad. Ye will see I'm right.'

With that Jeff walked out of the Post Office chuckling to himself.

Over the next few months more people began to talk about this World Cup. I discovered a replica trophy was in the Working Men's Club. Indeed, if every person who talked about it had a 'great grandfather who played in the team', then the team must have consisted of a hundred men. Like an itch that had to be scratched, the old researcher in me decided the matter had to be investigated. Surely Jeff could not be right?

So, began my research into the football history books and the discovery of a previously unknown archive that revealed the whole story.

THOMAS LIPTON

My first revelation was that indeed a trophy had been played for and was linked to a Thomas Lipton. Now that was a name I knew. He owned a shop in York Street, Belfast, when I was a lad. Many times, I had visited the shop with my granny - indeed everybody in Belfast knew the name Lipton. I therefore started my journey back in Ireland.

There I found the records for Thomas Lipton Senior, born at Shannock Mills near Clones in Northern Ireland in 1810. When he married Frances, they would have looked around Ireland in the 1830's and saw Ireland's Tithe War sweeping from the south to their Northern Ireland home. Destitution and poverty was spreading and Ireland was heading for an Drochshaol, literally 'the bad life', known elsewhere as the Irish Potato Famine. Just as Victoria was ascending to the British throne, they decided that they would leave their Clones family home and head for Scotland and a better life. However, it was not a story of great riches for the family, one report stated that Thomas senior never earned more than a pound a week (£128 in 2017).

The life of Thomas Lipton is an intriguing one which began in Hutchesontown when, in 1848, Thomas Johnston Lipton arrived, the youngest of five children. He attended St. Andrew's Parish School where he was found not to be of a great academic standard, however, he succeeded in mastering reading, writing and arithmetic. His attention was never on formal education and he longed to be free from school - later versions of his life described him growing up obsessed with yachts and racing model boats at High Fields near his home in Crown Street. It is there that he was supposed to have carved his first model boat, which was fully rigged, named *Shamrock* - a nod to his Irish roots. It was also claimed he and his friends formed a club to have yacht races and it is said that it was here that Thomas Lipton developed his competitive spirit and his passion for yachting.

His home is best described as a clean decent working class one, where his father worked as a porter, probably in a local warehouse. His first job was in a Glasgow shop where he earned 2s 6d a week (£38 2018) he soon looked for a rise in his wages and when refused he left and became a warehouse boy in the warehouse where his father worked. His ambition was seen in his promise to his mother that he would have *'a carriage and pair'* for her before long. There followed a number of jobs for Thomas, in which he either could not settle or in which he felt he was not being paid his worth. The sea, albeit a small one, entered Thomas' life, as he became a cabin boy with the Burns Line on the Glasgow to Belfast route. An incident on the boat led to him being accused of damaging a lamp and he was sacked. At seventeen he worked and scraped together enough to take steerage passage to New York determined to make a fortune. He worked in South Carolina where he was responsible for the finances and book-keeping for a small firm. This gave him a good understanding of running a business, then he moved on to work on a rice plantation, as a tramcar driver, then a fireman, and latterly, as a grocer's assistant in a New York department store, where he learned the art of trading.

This was not to be but he did raise a hundred pounds (£11,500 2018) and headed back to Glasgow, where he opened his first shop.

Lipton was a man of great theatricals, who was a pioneer of spectacular advertising and knew how to catch the public's eye. He used the exceptional talents of Willie Lockhart, a leading cartoonist, to produce eye-catching posters, many using the stereotypical images of the Irishman in his knee britches, long tailed coat with a shillelagh, driving pigs that were destined for the Lipton's stores. Lipton would even go the extent of getting real pigs and driving them through the streets, with ribbons on their tails and a banner proclaiming them as 'Lipton's Orphan's', the phrase used in the cartoons. He would organise competitions when stores opened, and employ outrageous events, such as rolling a massive cheese to a new shop, and in Nottingham even had an elephant attend an opening. Such was his flair that he would use to attract attention to his football events and draw the involvement of countries and their teams. Indeed, there was hardly a corner in the world that did not host a 'Lipton' trophy competition, whether for football, cricket, sailing, or racing. With such activities and publicity his grocery empire with its wealth and influence grew across the world, and he became a friend of Presidents, Queens and Kings.

Despite all this, Thomas would never forget his humble origins and these influenced his decisions and ambitions throughout his life. The sea and sailing became his passion. This passion, seen in his early model yacht racing, would see him at his most competitiveness, especially in the America's Cup. He made five attempts to win it from 1899 to 1930. He never did. The history records him during this period as 'the loveable loser', which reflects his spirit of encouraging the ambitions of the underdog. This spirit was most likely at the root of his part in the amazing tale that will unfold in this book. Thomas Lipton's desire to encourage was also seen in football. He had watched the very early games of England playing Scotland and this ignited a new enthusiasm. Lipton's own passion and drive were clearly seen in this game. He had to get involved.

WHERE DID FOOTBALL START?

It is right to set the context of Thomas Lipton's world tournament in the then world of modern football. The origins of the game are shrouded in the mists of history. It is thought to have been played in some form before 300 BC. During the *Han* and *Tsin* Dynasty's in China, around the second and third century BC, we find records in a military manual of a game called *Tsu' Chu*, this literally means 'kicking a stuffed leather ball with the feet'. It is interesting to note that during the Tang Dynasty in the 7th century, women began to play the game. Women's football is not such a modern idea after all! There was also a Japanese version later but this was less competitive and simply was a version of 'keepie uppie' in which the ball was passed in a circle by kicking, and it was not allowed to touch the ground.

The Greeks and Romans also had a ball game called *Episkyros* that has two sides that try to get the ball over a line defended by each team. The game would often be played in the nude. Not the best idea for football in an English winter! The use of hands was also permitted, as was violence; this aspect was particularly a feature of the Roman version, *Harpastum*. Whilst the terms and rules are not fully clear the ancient writers speak of the object to keep the ball from the opponents using feet and hands, throwing it over the heads of opponents. In many ways the description would indicate a more rugby style of play. Records of serious injuries show that it was not a beautiful game. It is interesting that a surviving depiction, on a monument, of the ball used, is 'sewed with a hexagonal pattern' similar to the modern ball.

What is clear is that a form of game with a ball, similar to football or rugby, was played all over the world – it was an international sport. It is also clear that the Roman legions would have brought their game of *Harpastum* to Britain, because of the aspect of fitness it gave to soldiers. However, it has to be noted that the game bore very little resemblance to football, as we know it, with the use of the feet being of little importance. It is to Britain we have to look for the emergence of modern football.

Football in the earliest centuries in Britain was disorganised, violent, chaotic and lawless. It had no limit on the number of players in a side and no time limit in a 'game's' duration. It was often played as a challenge between whole villages. A game could flow from a village street, through the square, over the hedges and into the fields. It was not always a welcomed sport. The Lord Mayor of London in 1314 banned the game within his city because of the chaos. Anyone breaking the ban was sent to prison. Edward III, Richard II, Henry IV and V all prohibited the game, because it took men away from military training. Even in Scotland the kings were opposed to the game, with James I stating in 1424: '..That no men play at football'

Elizabethan times saw a great interest in football. In Italy the game was very much brought into a more civilised and organised form. The image in the image section shows the game being played in a public square with a very well organised team layout.

The teams would be dressed in very elaborate costumes, prefiguring modern team strips. Football known as *Calcio* in Italy was no doubt observed by many from Britain on their world tours. The Elizabethan period saw many ideas from around the world being introduced to England.

Richard Mulcaster is an important figure at this time. He was one of the foremost teachers in England being connected with Cambridge, Oxford, Eton along with Taylors and St Paul's.

A great advocate of the arts and sport he would be familiar with Florence, an area where *Calcio* flourished. He would introduce refinements to football. These included organised teams or sides, referees, stress on using the '*legges*' and gave the name '*footeball*'. However, these refinements were not wide-spread and the football throughout the land was still a rough event. It remained a target for authorities who would bring in prohibitions, in places such as Manchester. The Puritans saw it as frivolous and corrupting. The turning point for football came in the 1800's.

HOME OF THE BEAUTIFUL GAME

There is no doubt that what became the modern game and a working man's sport began its evolution in the Public Schools of Britain. In the closed hard paved squares of many of these schools, it became evident that some discipline and rules were necessary. The old mob rule game no longer suited or could be played in the refined courtyards of Charterhouse, Rugby and Eton, among others. Furthermore, the rucks, scrums and mauls in which the ball could be touched and carried were not appropriate and this gave way to a more artful dribbling of the ball, using the feet. As the game became an important part of the school's curricula the need for standardisation and rules became evident. It was

Doctor Thomas Arnold of Rugby school who took the first steps in that direction. In those days the kicking of an opponent below the knee was permitted but he could not be held while his shins were kicked! Running with the ball held in the hand or arms was still allowed. William Webb Ellis is credited with setting the game of Rugby Football on its way, when he picked up the ball and ran with it, even though many had done it before him. It was at this point an evident split was ahead between those who wanted the use of hands and arms and those who wanted feet only.

It was in the rarefied atmosphere of Cambridge where definitive steps were taken to bring a greater standardisation of the many forms of football that had sprung up. The majority wanted to ban the practice of shin kicking, tripping and the other rougher expressions of the game, as then played. It was also the majority's view that there should be no touching or carrying of the ball in arms or hand. It became clear that three particular forms of football would emerge: Rugby Football, Gaelic Football and Modern Football. On the 26th October 1863, in the Freemason's Tavern in London, twelve team representatives held a meeting and agreed a set of regulations that would govern their games together. This in fact was the founding of the Football Association. There would still be struggles ahead to bring others into the fold, but the game was now set on its modern path. The formation of the Football League would follow in 1888 when William McGregor brought together the twelve foundation teams. The Northern League would be formed the following year.

Internationally the British game was very insular and it was only through the travels of the British abroad that the modern game spread to other countries. The first true International match was played in 1872 between England (Team members were drawn from various clubs) and Scotland (Team members were from Queen's Park), although it was not an 'official' event as the Scottish Association had not yet been formed. In 1883-4 the four British home nations, organised a tournament, which saw the four 'international teams' from each country involved. In the 1900 Olympics football was introduced as a demonstration sport with France, Belgium and England taking part. Upton Park from London was the English team who topped the table at that event. It is notable that in 1904 in Paris, when FIFA was founded, no English,

Scottish or Irish national associations were involved. This throws light on the main topic of this book when England refused to join in Lipton's tournaments throughout the world. However, the English association was, with great reluctance, brought into the fold. They would be responsible for the organisation of the Olympic football that took place in 1908. There were five international teams represented: Great Britain, Denmark, Netherlands, France and Sweden. The Great British Team won the event and was composed of amateur platers. Football was now truly rooted throughout the British Isles, with teams being formed all over the country. Very quickly English teams began to travel abroad. We find that South America had visits from Southampton (1904), Nottingham Forest (1905), Everton and Tottenham (1909), Corinthians (1910 & 1913), Swindon Town (1912) and Exeter City (1914). Argentina and Uruguay regularly competed in 'international games'.

Sir Thomas Lipton also took a keen interest in football in that region. In 1905 he donated a trophy to be contested by the two teams. The *Copa de Caridad Lipton* was a trophy that had to be contested by the teams using only native players. Uruguay, the team that won FIFA's first world cup in 1930, were also the first to win the *Copa de Caridad Lipton*.

In 1908 Italy was the venue for an 'international' trophy, *Torneo Internazionale Stampa Sportiva*. This was called the First International Tournament by the Italians. However, it was dominated by Italy who held a qualifying round among its home club teams. Only Switzerland, Italy, Germany and France were involved, sending over their own championship teams. The success of this made Lipton aware of the need to involve English teams and he set his sights on another tournament in Turin – this time he would personally organise a team from England.

Martin Connolly

LIPTON AND THE VILLAGE AT THE CROSSROADS

E arlier, in 1899 Queen Victoria knighted Thomas Lipton, appropriately, at her Isle of Wight residence just a few miles from the yachting centre of Cowes. In that year the second Boer War was raging. Here in England the recruitment of men revealed a working population that was very badly fed. This prompted the then Princess Alexandra to approach Thomas Lipton with his grocery empire to help. The Alexandra Trust was set up with Lipton making a generous donation and agreeing to provide food at cheap prices to the poor and unemployed. He also was aware that the miner's strikes had devastated the mining community and had gave instructions to his many stewards throughout the United Kingdom to give free tea to mining families. One such distribution would certainly have happened at the mining village of West Auckland in County Durham, which had its own mine as well as others nearby. The village also had a football team in a local league and the Northern League, which ran in the area had a referee who was one of the stewards Lipton had instructed. He would know of the many football teams in the Auckland's area.

It was in 1901 when King Edward VII ascended the throne; he made Thomas Lipton a Knight Commander of the Royal Victorian Order. The King had long been fond of Lipton through yachting and the award was in recognition of his charitable work with the King's wife, now Queen Alexandra, as well as his sporting activity.

In 1908 Sir Thomas was informed he was to become a member of both the Grand Order of the Crown of Italy and the Order of St. Sava (to which he was officially inducted in 1910). This news was greeted with great appreciation by Sir Thomas and his response was to offer a football trophy that would be competed for in Turin, Italy in 1909.

> *'The English millionaire sir Thomas Lipton is very talented at separating his encouraging work for the benefit of business*

and trade and also for the benefit of sport. He is the lucky owner of the famous tea plantation and won fame for his country with this trade. In order to promote Italian football, he wanted to offer us a lavish trophy worth two thousand lira, specially crafted by the firm Goldsmiths and Silversmiths of London.'

It was simply called 'The Sir Thomas Lipton Trophy'. This event was known in Italy as the Second International Tournament. This decision to donate a trophy, led to a story that had the quality of one that could have appeared in the pages of Roy of the Rovers!

    The village of West Auckland was on a crossroads that existed long before Roman times, with a road going to what became the Binchester Roman fort. It was first mentioned in the Bolden Book of 1183. Its lands were under the Lordship of the Prince Bishop of Durham and supplied labour for his other lands. He took the tithe of their work. The village had at its height nine hostelries to accommodate the travellers through the crossroads. The village was touched by the many wars that had raged over the centuries in England – the various antagonists would have passed through it. The village would have seen the Brigantine peoples, the Celts, The Vikings (They named the local river, *Gaunless*, meaning 'useless'), the Romans, Royalists and the Roundheads, not to mention the various Scottish invaders who often visited as far as nearby Barnard Castle to claim territory. Mention is made of the Eden's, one of West Auckland's famous families in a history article, in the 1831 Gentleman's Magazine:

> *'At Bildenshaw, near West Auckland, aged 99, John Goundry, farmer. He remembered the Rebellion, and seeing the Duke of Cumberland, whose carriage broke down between Piercebridge and West Auckland, owing to the bad state of the roads. The Duke was*

supplied with a new carriage and horses, by Sir Robert Eden – grandfather to the present Baronet – who then lived at West Auckland'

Sir Anthony Eden, a descendent of this Eden family, became Prime Minister in 1955.

The village, nestling in a quiet valley of South Durham, had beneath it a very precious commodity – coal. Durham was the first area to be recorded as having commercial coal pits. The Bolden Book mentions a pit at Escombe just up the road from West Auckland. In 1530 John Leland visited the area and commented on the pits and the sending of coal to Richmond and North Yorkshire. This coal would have been moved along the 'Coal Road' which was noted, in 1457, as running from Darlington through West Auckland to Piercebridge. It was also mentioned in an Act of Parliament in 1807. George Stephenson, in 1823, built the first cast iron railway bridge spanning a river, over the *Gaunless* at West Auckland, to facilitate the movement of coal. Fordyce, writing in 1857, records that the labouring population of West Auckland was mainly engaged in coal mining. It was from this community of miners a small club was formed.

The first known club formed was reported by The North Eastern Daily Gazette on the 4th September 1891. It was called the West Auckland Tradesmen's Football Club. In 1892 we find The West Auckland Wesleyans playing in the Teesside Minors League. In 1893 we read of a friendly being played at Stockton between West Auckland and Stockton. Stockton ran out winners, with six goals to nil score. The game was reported as being played in very cold weather and badly attended. It was after this we find the club referred to as West Auckland Football Club.

At the Annual General Meeting of the Auckland and District Football League on the 9th of June 1894, the Northern Echo reports West Auckland being listed as a member of the league. They are in the first division of a three-division league. In that year (July) the same paper reports that the club needs financial help, from the more well-off people of West Auckland, for its survival. By 1896 the team is playing in the Wear Valley League and progress to the South Durham Alliance in 1900. In 1905 they move to the Mid Durham League and in 1908 they join the prodigious Northern League, after many attempts.

The 08/09 season was not remarkable, finishing the season in tenth place out of twelve. They won six matches, drew four and lost twelve. Surely this team cannot take on any sort of international competition and win? This is where the fairy tale begins.

WAS IT A CASE OF MISTAKEN IDENTITY?

Despite many theories that suggest the Football Association in England were asked to take part in the tournament, a search of its archive has found no record of any invite to take part in the 1909 tournament in Turin. They have also no record of any team being asked to go to the event. Let us therefore deal with a myth that has circulated over the years. Was Woolwich Arsenal the intended team for the original invitation to take part in the Turin tournament? The categorical answer is 'no'. *La Stampa*, who organised the event, was clear about the team they had written to. Their official Italian newspaper reports before the Tournament was held states:

'...West Auckland which belongs to the most important Amateur Federation in North England.'

Furthermore, they were not particularly interested in a top English team. La Stampa reported:

'If we claimed the English team that will compete in our tournament is the best from foggy Britain, it would be presumptuous and maybe even foolish. In fact, in a country where thousands and thousands of football clubs are flourishing, you cannot categorically claim to be a team that is a cut above the rest. Because of the multiple championships and cup competitions, which at times are perhaps more important than the aforementioned

championships, successful teams often win easily one day, only to be defeated by teams of the same standard the next. England is the home, if not the place of origin, of the dynamism of the Football Association. All of the teams that can barely keep their place at the bottom of the Championship table are definitely superior to any of our club teams and other foreign ones'.

From these two statements there is clear proof that the Italians knew it was a team from the Northern League that they were getting.

However, was West Auckland F C the intended Auckland team? Before we try to answer that, let us consider the most plausible account of an Auckland's team involvement in the tournament. Sir Thomas Lipton, as we have seen, was well acquainted with miners and the hardships that were involved in the industry. He had used his resources to support them and knew that across the country many miners took part in football, another of Sir Thomas' passions. One of Sir Thomas' employees, who assisted in the distribution of aid to miners in the Durham area, was also a referee in the Northern League. Sir Thomas was very familiar with Bishop Auckland, as he had corresponded with a lady, Ethel Ion, who had sent him a pen and ink sketch in 1903.

Having this familiarity with Bishop Auckland, it is highly likely that Sir Thomas had asked his employee to recommend a team from the Northern League, which was the oldest and a highly respected league with a great history, even in 1908/9. But what team did he recommend. This is where the matter gets interesting. The organisers of the event give a detailed list of the background of the invited team. The expected English team:

> *...had won against international teams.*
> *... belongs to Northern England Division.*
> *...are from County Durham.*

...in 1908/09 Season they won Wear Valley League.

...had played in the South Durham Alliance.

...had played in the Mid Durham League.

...were in Final of Durham' Amateurs Cup.

...were in the Semi-Final of English Amateur Championship (Forfeited match because of injury to player against South Bank)

...beat South Bank 4 to 2 in 1908/9

..had beaten Northern Nomads, Stockton and Darlington.

The Italians had the name, 'West Auckland Football Club', but they were mistaken in which club that was. There was an Auckland team who were experienced in going abroad - to Belgium and Holland. Their goalkeeper had experience when he played for England in France in

1906. There was a team who had won a league in the 1908/9 season. There was a team who had been in various amateur cups. There was a team who had beaten South Bank 4 - 2 in 1908/9 and who had beaten Northern Nomads (3 - 1), Stockton (3 - 0) and Darlington (2 - 0). They were in at the foundation of the Northern League and were a very successful team in that league. That team was Bishop Auckland.

West Auckland had their first league derby against Bishop in 1908 when they achieved a 1 - 1 draw. They had played in the various Wear Valley and Durham leagues up to that point in their history. Whatever the communication that had come from England, it had described Bishop Auckland as the team to go to Turin. However, and no one is sure of the reason, it was West Auckland Football Club to whom the invitation went. We can conclude that there was a case of mistaken identity, but as we will discover, that gave a great opportunity to a team of courageous miners to ascend from the pit and rise to glory and to walk tall into football history.

THE 1909 TOURNAMENT

The reasons for the tournament in Turin were made clear by the Italian organisers.

> *'We aim to promote the game of football, striving to increase its popularity in our country; to convince even the most reluctant of people to take to the pitch; to unite side by side the strongest foreign players with our promising stars; to offer our young sportsmen an opportunity to closely admire and observe the talent and tactics of the game in countries beyond the Alps; to*

> *improve the progress already made by our compatriots in the last year, by holding matches between Italians and foreign players.'*

There we have it - the motivation behind our great football venture. The Italians were keen to improve the national team and involvement in football by more men. They were prosaic in their hopes:

> 'The presence of this elite group of champions from the green lands of Albion is without precedent in Italy and will write one of the most beautiful pages in the history of the renaissance of our historical game of Calcio'

As noted above, *Calcio* was the Italian form of football, played in Florence. They were also looking to foreign players, particularly British, to develop and train Italians in the art of the game. This idea of including foreigners in the national game, including the national team, was a cause of great division in Italy. The Tournament organisers were effusive in their hopes:

> *'Easter is drawing nearer. The tournament, which takes place on the 11th and 12th of April, is fast approaching, and as it is such an important event, everything must be meticulously prepared. Our 2nd international tournament must live up to the standards set by the 1st, while also giving palpable proof of its gravitas, professionalism and importance to those participating. We also offer the competitors an abundance of prizes, like no other sporting event has before.'*

As noted above the *Torneo Internazionale Stampa Sportiva* was contested in 1908 between Italy, France,

Switzerland and Germany with Torino winning the tournament, beating the Swiss team *Servette* in the final. However, the organisers felt that for a truly international tournament, a team from England was needed. However, all was not happy within the Italian football community and the division within the football federation caused the Juventus team to refuse to take part in the Tournament. The Italian press was caustic:

> *'The withdrawal of the Juventus players was motivated only by personal rivalries that emerged at the last minute between some members of Torino F.C.. Sadly, we have observed once more how all too easily those who could contribute a lot to a team's success as part of an initiative such as ours, prefer, to the detriment of football's progress in Italy (still relatively modest) to spread inappropriate gossip. Everybody muses upon the*

ripples of such gossip and fosters one idea: to be able to offer the Italian clubs an opportunity to reaffirm their own importance.'

The Italian team was finally composed of players from Torino F.C. and Piemonte F.C. and surprisingly three foreign players, one being English. He was Arthur Rodgers, who had played for Nottingham and was now playing for Torino. The referee would also be an English man, Mr Godley, who had refereed in England and was now a trainer for Juventus. The scene was set for an historic football event.

It is fair to say that the West Auckland Team did not get the appropriate coverage in the British press, as they set out on their amazing journey. Indeed, the Northern Echo reported on the expected England versus Holland match scheduled for Easter Monday that year and also had an 'Easter Tours' section which focused on Bishop Auckland's visit to Belgium alongside South Bank and Stockton's visit to the London area. No mention was made about West Auckland! Bishop won their competition abroad and received coverage on their return lauding their victory, but nothing for the lads from West. This probably reflects the view that not much was expected to be achieved by the team.

One can only imagine what Syd Barron (this is how his name appears in many old documents), West Auckland's club secretary, must have thought when he was handed a letter that came from Italy. He would have known of the foreign trips of other clubs in the area, but to receive an invitation to play in Turin, Italy must have been a shock. In 1909 West Auckland were strapped for cash. They had opted out of travelling to some games because of the expense, so a trip to Italy would be madness. However, how could any football club turn down such an invite? The Italian organisers tell us that a reply was indeed received in Turin.

'The English team we have signed up will be worthier than any other pseudo-tournament involving mediocre clubs not in order with the International

Federation dispositions, in glaringly demonstrating to our friends from outside Turin that La Stampa Sportiva is completely unbiased when creating its few but magnificent and renowned sports events'.

Not only would the team play in the Tournament, they were also to play other Italian teams:

> 'It is well-known that every City and club genuinely cares about engaging with and competing against foreign players during the Easter holidays both for sports and, mainly, for financial reasons. Motivated by a sense of charity and good sportsmanship, when we previously excluded those clubs which were not from Turin, we also immediately thought about placating them by organising a direct match with

the best team in the tournament: the English team.

In fact, in accepting the English team, we especially worried about finding a club that could spend a whole week in Italy after our two-day tournament, securing it to play three other matches against our footballer friends from Vercelli, Milan and Genoa.

The arrival of a British club in Italy for the very first time was too important and valuable for us not to think about sharing this honour with Turin players' colleagues from Milan, Genoa and Vercelli. For this reason, we went through long negotiations and we succeeded in making the very strong West Auckland Team compete against Pro Vercelli in Vercelli on Thursday April 15th, against Genoa Cricket in Genoa on Saturday 17th and against Unione Sportiva Milanese in Milan on Sunday 18th.'

The glowing tributes show that the Italians respected the English team and expected great things from them. Despite the original mistaken identity, they would not be disappointed.

Miles Coverdale Stocks Barron, to give Syd his full name, was a Colliery Manager in 1901. By 1911 he had become an architect and surveyor in the building trade. Born at Waterhouses in 1871, he married Mary Ann Bird in 1893. In 1909, when he received the letter from Turin, he was living at St Helen's Auckland with Mary Ann, his son Percy and two daughters, Muriel and Maisie, who had been born in the previous year. By all accounts he was a jovial man and a great motivator of men. His management of the team no doubt was heavily influenced by his skills as a manager at the pit. At 37 years of age, to see a bit of the world would have been an exciting opportunity that he would not want to miss. To combine it with his passion for football made it certain that he would get a team together to take up the challenge.

As noted earlier, the team had just come into the Northern League. Having only won six out of twenty-two matches, to be told they were going to take part in an international tournament, would have initially brought a grin to the faces of the tough miners. Add to this the severe lack of finances the club was experiencing and even the most enthusiastic team member would have a certain scepticism of taking on such a venture but take it on they did.

The team Syd put together was drawn from a pool of players from around the region. It would include some 'guests'. In goal would be Jimmy Dickenson, a 29-year-old - unmarried, he was born in Cockfield. He worked as a hewer at the pit and was a regular for the team. Three brothers, Tommy, Bob and Frank Gill were selected. Bob was 31 and he was married to Margaret with five children at that time, the youngest being just a year old. Tommy was 33 and married to Mary Alice. He had three children, and like his brother his youngest was also just a year old. Both of them were hewers at the local pit. Frank was 24 and at the time of the trip was single. He originally worked underground at the pit hauling trolleys, but by 1911 he is running a 'Fryed Fish Shop' on Front Street in West Auckland. These lads loved their football and always made sure they had a match every week, sometimes even two. They regularly played for Eldon Albion Football Club and had won trophies with that team. Frank had a contract with Sunderland AFC for the season 1908/9, but Sunderland archives cannot find any record of him actually playing for them. Their elder brother John William, who did not make the trip, was heavily involved in Eldon A F C, and was involved in the early days of purchasing a ground for Albion to use. According to Tommy they were asked to go on the Italian trip because others couldn't raise the necessary money or were not keen on the journey. Frank, Robert and Tommy paid their own way without having to resort to borrowing or selling off any goods. Photos of those days shows Tommy was used to picking up trophies.

John (Jock) Greenwell, born in Crook, was 25 and also a hewer at the pit. He was single and by all accounts very sharp on the ball. He played for Crook Town and as we will see went on to greater things in the football world.

Rob Jones was born Robert Ovington in Newfield, County Durham. At 26 he was a hewer at the colliery and was married to Edith. He had no children at that time. Charles Parker Hogg (had the nickname 'Dirty'), born in West Auckland, he was 29 years old and married to Bertha. A stalwart of the team, he had two young sons as he prepared for his 1909 journey. He was a muscular blacksmith and his strength and stamina would be needed in Turin. As far as the author can tell, Ben Whitttingham was a hewer from Shildon who was single and in his early twenties. Joseph Douglas Crawford was 28 and single. Born in Bishop Auckland, he was an architect who probably worked with Syd Barron. Bob Guthrie was a regular in the early days of the team, but few records exists about him. Alf Gubbins was a 24-year-old railway shunter, born at Shildon. Married to Jane he would celebrate with the birth of a baby girl on his return.

John 'Jock' Jones was 24, born at St Andrews Auckland and single. He was a colliery blacksmith. He would marry his wife Emily the following year, after his return from Italy. David Rees (Ticer) Thomas was 35 years old and a hewer at the local pit. He was born in Corbridge, Burslem in Staffordshire and lived in West Auckland.

Married to Mary Ethel, he had two sons and two daughters when he set of for Turin.

Syd Barron was well aware of the financial burden that would be placed on many of the players. Bob Chamberlain, born in West Auckland, was the treasurer and he would know well how bad the finances really were. He was a stonemason who moved into the general building trade, as a contractor and had the job of making sure the trip could happen. Whilst a number of the team were able to contribute, it still was a challenge for the team as a whole. The reports that appeared later of selling furniture was laughed at by a son of Charlie Hogg, who commented that they could not have sold furniture because they had none to sell! The average wage for a miner was around £85 a year (it is hard to be exact on wages in those days, as there were different calculations and deductions etc.) that would be about £9500 today (2018).

We have to remember there were no cheap airlines and the journey would be made by trains and boat. Then there was food and accommodation, not forgetting the loss of wages. With all that in mind the decision to take on the trip was a courageous one and demonstrates the passion for the game the team had. The Italian organisers were well aware of the financial implications, even for their own Italian players, and commented on this in their reports:

'Few sporting events require such difficult and laborious planning and such vast spending as a football tournament. In fact, since football's spirit lies in its team of 11 players, it's easy to see why bringing together more football teams to compete - from England, Germany and Switzerland - in an Italian city is so expensive. Seeing as the most effort and money is being poured into creating a venture that highlights the importance of the event. Therefore, it is logical to conclude that the international football tournament banned for the

second year running by La Stampa Sportiva will be an extremely important sporting reunion, envied by not only other cities in Italy, but from abroad too. The fact that we will have among us an English team, for the first time given that football is flourishing in Italy, shows the truth in our assertion.'

They were worried about finding an English club who could afford to come to Italy for a week. The team therefore had to rely on getting donations from local businesses and some of the team resorted to selling their own valuables to finance the expedition to Turin. The Italian organisers did not have the names of the West Auckland players in advance when they outlined the players of each team:

For Italy:
Goal keeper: Faroppa, in defence: Bollinger, Capra, the midfield

was Engler, Rodgers, Capello D and the forwards, Zuffi J, Zuffi S, Bernardo F, Simonazzi and Debernardi.

For Germany:

Mr Karl Schlütter (goalkeeper), Eugen Lessing, Franz Krezdorn, Eduard Murr, Eugen Munk, Hermann Renz, Ludwig Rossi, Karl Benk, Karl Burger, Eugen Kipp and Otto Gramm.

For Switzerland:

Karl Arbenz (goalkeeper), Henri Müller (Captain), Bachmann Heinrich (backs), Albert Nemveiler, Hans Walter III. Egli Karl (half-backs) Ernst Walter I, Koblet Ulrich, Reich and Lang (forwards).

West Auckland was the only team whose players did not get listed in the official release of teams and players. The announcement simply states that West Auckland 'wanted to participate with their best footballers'. This in part could have been due to the confusion over West Auckland and Bishop Auckland. The report further goes on to state,

> 'The rigorous training the English athletes do when they take part in an important international competition such as our Tournament leaves us in no doubt of the perfect shape of the team who will defend the English colours'

For the miners of West Auckland, the rigorous training was mainly down a pit and they would prove that they indeed were very capable of defending the English colours! The photograph that they published of the team captains, after their arrival, shows the West Auckland Captain is the only one with his country's flag.

The team travelled to London and from there caught the boat train through to Paris and finally ended up at Turin's Porta Nuova station, one of the most beautiful in Europe and a lot grander than Bishop Auckland or Darlington's!

One Italian commentator was not greatly impressed by their dress sense when he saw them after their first match.

> *'Seeing them like this in their football shirts, to tell the truth, didn't give a much better impression than seeing them in casual dress at Porta Nuova Station'.*

He obviously did not appreciate the journey the lads had undertaken.

THE FIRST DAY OF THE TOURNAMENT

Turin had not seen excitement like this for a football match before. This was largely due to the participation of an English team. From before 2 p.m. the crowd had started to gather. The Turin ground had been decked with flags of every nation. A band was playing upbeat marching music. The crowd was dressed in a range of great costumes. When the gates were opened the crowd flooded in to fill the spacious seats and standing space at the front. Around 2.45 p.m. the dignitaries began to arrive to take their reserved seating, which was surrounded by the large crowd. First there was Montu, the Marquis de Ferrero President of the Italian

Football Association, Tacconis, representing the Mayor of Turin, then entered, followed by vice-consuls from Switzerland and France, who were then followed by a host of football and civil greats. They were dressed in their finest, with the ladies being noted as having their tight corsets and wearing vivid spring colours, reflective of the Easter season and the hot Italian day. The Tournament's organising committee were seen actively ensuring the crowd and dignitaries were comfortable and that everything was in place for the great event. The Municipal Guards and the Carabinieri, with their Chief of Police, Bessi, mounted on his horse, provided security and confidence to the eager crowds. It was a truly magnificent setting for an expected magnificent Tournament of Football.

Italy v Switzerland

On the dot of 2.45 p.m. the music stopped and the Italian team ran on to the pitch. They had their strip of white jerseys, hooped with the stripes of the Italian colours, which sent the crowd into raptured applause. The Swiss followed in black and blue jerseys. Both teams appeared animated and eager to get on with play. The Swiss were their country's national champions and were expected to out-perform the Italian mixed side. The same Italian side had taken on another Swiss team, *Chaux de Fons*, the previous Thursday and had come away with a credible nil, nil draw. They were known to have expressed determination to fight to the bitter end for a victory against Winterthur. An Englishman, Clark and an Italian, Perruzi were linesmen, and Godley the referee. A quick sharp blast of his whistle got the game started.

The Swiss had the kick off. The sun was blinding and behind the Italians, giving them an initial edge. They soon had the ball away from the Swiss and were pressing hard on the Swiss goal. The Italians were showing some brilliant dribbling skills and seemed to take the Swiss by surprise. The Swiss pushed the Italians back, but they were not giving in easily and there was another Italian raid on the Swiss goal.

Fresia, for the Italians, took the ball and with a very elegant pass on the thirteenth minute, placed it at the feet of Debernardi who thumped it towards the Swiss Goal. It bounced just in front of the diving Swiss keeper, shooting over him and cracking hard against the crossbar. Bernardo, moving like a rocket, hit the rebounding ball with his knee and watched it hammer against the back of the Swiss net. This sent the home crowd into ecstatic applause and cheering which was joined in by the watching West Auckland team.

The goal spurred both teams into a very energetic period of the match, with both sets of defenders being called into action. Just before the half hour, Lang for Winterthur was left unmarked close to the Italian goal. With a cracking shot, he thumped the ball past the leaping Faroppa to level the score. The remainder of the half was an exciting tussle between two teams trying to get the upper-hand. Simonazzi almost gave the Italians the lead with a terrific header that just soared over the Swiss crossbar.

The second half brought an exciting period of play, with great agile football. Both teams fought hard, with the game flowing into both team's half of the pitch. Defence and forwards played their part in giving the crowd a great spectacle of football. By the time of the final whistle, the score had remained the same. The referee and organisers agreed to continue play to a definite win by either team. Two further periods of twenty minutes then ensued, with both teams showing amazing stamina in the heat. The Swiss forced hard, making many attempts on goal, but the brilliance of Faroppa, kept them at bay. The play had been going on now for two hours and nine minutes when the Italian Bollinger was in his own penalty area and the ball hit him on the arm. Godley blew for a penalty. Lang stepped up for the Swiss and with what can only be described as an unstoppable shot, smashed home the winning goal. After one hundred and thirty minutes of play, both teams left the field fatigued, with the Swiss, Winterthur, 2-1 winners. The Italian team fought hard and deserved a great deal of credit, in their struggle with the Swiss champions.

The Italian reporters of the match cannot be faulted for their passion and romance, even with football. One over-excited reported wrote of this match:

> *'Journalism is an ugly profession and, although this is no revelation, it's good to remind yourself of this sometimes. Like all ugly professions however, it gives you some satisfaction – a small one, but a pleasure nonetheless. Today I had one such pleasure whilst watching a girl at the football match flirting as if she was at a horse race. The satisfaction was, I admit, fleeting, but as I had hoped for something similar to happen in the last article I relished in it, very happy to have seen for myself the enthusiasm that football matches can sometimes produce. Indeed, at one point,*

while the grass was blazing with sunlight and the furious multi-coloured struggle for the ball intensified, I saw the man, in the heat of the moment, reaching almost instinctively for her hand in nervous excitement.

A shout came from the many voices in the crowd; a cry that faded into a bitter murmur. The two teams came together for a moment, then dispersed in a boisterous mass and lined up in front of the Italian goal. The public were silent, motionless and tense and his hand, again in the heat of the moment, instinctively clasped around her waist.

I would have liked to go up to the girl and whisper that it was time to give a 'penalty kick' or at least a 'penalty' but I held back these profound thoughts as I was convinced she would kick me, probably repeatedly.'

England versus Germany

It was the same reporter who gave an account of his meeting with a West Auckland miner before the match, which sums up the encounter between the Durham miners and the Italian public:

'..with notable courage, I hurriedly scraped together my limited knowledge of English and chose my victim in the form of a big, strapping man who was as plump as a well-fed cook. I approached him nonchalantly and once more chewed over my terrible sentence. I grabbed him by the shirt and, with immense difficulty, I managed to ask him: "Are you hoping you'll win?" –

And I swallowed something, maybe shame. The English man looked at me, turned towards the pitch and then slowly replied:
"Oh... yes!"
After a pause, I started again:
"It's hot isn't it?"
"Oh... yes!"
Yet another silence and, impressively, I managed to formulate another sentence which I fired at him shamelessly:
"So, if you're sensitive to the heat, you'll lose"
"Oh... yes!" – He replied, looking truly offended.
But no, I thought – this time he was mistaken; he should have said no. I kept looking at him, unsure whether I should keep up this interesting conversation or cut it short. For the reputation of

Italian journalism, I thought it better to leave with dignity.
"Alright... Good-bye!"
"Good bye." And the English footballer – who looked more like a red-faced cook than a sportsman – turned his back on me.'

It was five minutes past five on Easter Sunday the 11th of April 1909, when Bob Guthrie led his team onto the pitch at Turin. For this match the German's team strip was almost identical to West Auckland's and the German team had to wear plain white shirts. The press reports comment that the Germans were *'all handsome solidly built blonde men'* whilst the West Auckland men were *'clean shaven English [are] rather small and undersized'*. Apparently, they aroused much attention and curiosity from the Italian spectators who were seeing them for the first time. The match kicked off at ten past five. Within minutes these small undersized Englishmen were *'bulldozing'* their way towards the German goal.

West Auckland were lively and energetic passing with superb precision and deft in their touches. The forwards were a well-oiled machine competing and decisive in their play. Very quickly four corners had been awarded to West Auckland but the greater height of the Germans prevented any scoring. However, the English team's superiority in the match soon showed. Gubbins dribbled the ball to the centre of the pitch and was quickly challenged by the German defenders. Dropping back into his own half he smoothly passed the ball to Crawford who was on the right wing. Crawford was quite nippy and took the ball forward slotting into the path of Ben Whittingham, who wasted no time in thumping it into the German net. The crowd who were curious at the entrance of the West Auckland team were now amazed at the lively and elegant play that was happening on the pitch and responded with much applause. One Italian reporter wrote, *'The superiority of the English was quickly revealed as they continued to threaten their opponents with an almost thundering game of speed and elegant precision'*.

Crawford was then injured in a clash with a German defender and had to leave the pitch. The English team continued with ten men, with four forwards pushing high into the German half. Despite being a man down West Auckland remained dominant:

> *This handicap quickly made itself known to the astonishing five forwards. The vacancy was quite evident, but despite being one man down, the superiority of the black and whites continued.*

The plucky English team drew a penalty from the Germans. Dickenson came from his goal to take the kick and made no mistake in putting it past the German Goalkeeper, Lessing. The Italian report goes on:

> *'But what can be said is that despite the German team's best efforts and a truly top-class performance, West Auckland continued to outdo them. However, they only succeeded to score a second goal towards the end of the first half, with a*

penalty kick from the English goalkeeper.'

The game was noted for the violence and rough tactics of the Stuttgart team, in contrast to the lively elegance, of West Auckland. The German team relied on heavy tackling and pushing and tried everything to distract the West Auckland lads. They in contrast, focussed on the ball not the player and as a result maintained a disciplined and efficient flow to the game. The game, even though it was played in the evening, was quite challenging for the English team as it was very hot and the players unused to these conditions. Their victory was all the more applauded as the German goalkeeper was described as magnificent. In fact, the reports claim that no other keeper could have stopped the goals the West Auckland team had scored. As the West Auckland team left the pitch, it was to the ringing of praise and applause for a great performance.

During the match, a reporter wrote, '*they had become elastic, flexible, and agile as rubber, almost as if new blood rushed through their proud bodies*'. A final newspaper summary wrote of the West Auckland team:

'The English team's game was impeccable, elegant, extremely lively yet agile. The German team's style, by comparison, was rather more violent. Their defence strategy involved pushing and a constant repositioning of players, and their attack consisted of forceful passes sometimes from one winger to another. The English were accustomed to focusing on the ball and not the player, and therefore found themselves somewhat unsettled by this Teutonic violence, which was the only reason why the English were not able to score a higher number of goals.

Nevertheless, the English team's attack was strong – their goalkeeper didn't have to block a single shot – but they did little else as they were unaccustomed to playing in such heat, and were missing a player, which is key for a squad that relies so heavily on teamwork.

The English team's abundant headers and their decisiveness when in a good position to take a shot, was something both beautiful and innovative. The German goalkeeper, too, was simply magnificent, beyond praise, and certainly no one else would have been able to block the dozens of shots fired at him by the English.'

The scene was now set for a great final between the Swiss and the English.

THE SECOND DAY OF THE TOURNAMENT

It was Easter Monday the 12th March. The spectators were assembling for the first match of the day between Italy and Germany. The crowd was not as large as on the Sunday but appeared as vocal and keen to watch the match. Because both teams had been beaten yesterday, they were both desperate for a win. The Italian team particularly were looking for a victory in front of a home crowd. At 3 p.m. exactly Mr Godley blew his whistle and the Italian team wasted no time in attacking the German goal. The German defended well, especially Lessing and Krezdorn. They pushed the Italians back into their own half. As, against West Auckland, the German side was very physical and tough. However, the Italians being more agile, and indeed elegant, persisted in their attack. In the fifteenth minute, an Italian half-back in trying to prevent a German charge on his goal, accidently handled the ball.

The referee had on hesitation in awarding the German team a free kick. With a well taken shot, the ball was sent sailing into the Italian goal area. The German forward had the height and was left unmarked and had no difficulty in heading the ball straight into the net.

The Italian team could have dropped their heads at this point but the goal had the opposite effect. Immediately they were once again pressing the German defence. In the thirty-fifth minute the pressure succeeded. After another free kick by Bollinger, the ball fell at the feet of Bernardi who ran with the ball, as if it was attached to his feet. The big German half back charged toward him intent of using his physical bulk to prevent his progress, but he smoothly passed the ball to Debernardi, dodging the tackle. Debernardi waiting near the goal and stayed onside. He took the ball with ease and with a great first touch, slammed it into the German net.

Having pulled back a goal, the crowd were applauding and encouraging the Italian team. At half time the score was still level. The first thirty minutes of the second half saw the match sway to and fro, as both teams looked for the second goal. It was then that the Italians got the upper-hand and the ball was slotted into the German goal by Simonazzi. The celebrations were cut short as the referee blew for off-side and the shocked Italian team regrouped for another surge. Three minutes later the ball was quickly recovered by the Italians and they swept once more to the attack.

A beautifully placed ball found the head of Simonazzi and in the thirty-third minute he again placed the ball firmly in the German goal. This time it stood. The rest of the game was played with tough challenges from the Germans and an Italian team who were not prepared to yield their advantage. The German team had played their part well but the Italians were too nimble and sharper. Capra, Bollinger, Fresia and Simonazzi were highly skilled and a credit to their team. After the final whistle the Germans were graceful in defeat and congratulated the Italian team on their performance. All eyes now turned to the final. The performances of Germany and Italy in their match confirmed that Winterthur and West Auckland well deserved to be called the best and strongest teams of the Tournament. Both had come through their heat with skill and panache and promised to deliver a great final.

THE GRAND FINAL

The two teams from England and Switzerland were described as the strongest squads of the tournament. There were huge expectations of the English dressed in their black and white strip. After the injury to Crawford, they had recovered and played their full team. Our intrepid Italian reporter was again on the scene:

> *'The English lived up to the high expectations. I saw the friend I met yesterday, the sportsman who looks like a well-fed cook. I greeted him sincerely, but he laughed sinisterly in reply, gravely taking off a panama hat, which was undoubtedly English,*

but with an elegant African style. My friend and his companions seemed not to be very concerned about their elegance, if at all. They only acquired a gazelle-like agility as they were playing and passing the ball like brave squirrels – everyone except my friend. You could say anything about him, except, quite frankly, that he is light on his feet.'

West Auckland ran onto the pitch in their striped jerseys. From the very beginning the English team pressured the Swiss goal. After six minutes the penalty area was a crowded place and the Swiss committed a foul on the West Auckland forward. There was then a well-rehearsed dummy that enabled the Swiss goalkeeper to be fooled. It appeared that a particular player was going to run up for the kick, when Bob Jones suddenly took a run at the ball and hammered it into the Swiss net. The remainder of the team ran to the scorer and celebrated the goal with many handshakes. The game continued at a fast pace. The West Aucklander's (described by reporters as scrawny) were often knocked to the ground by the very athletic Swiss players. The newspaper reports describe the scene:

> *'The Swiss Black and Blues played a rather heavy, sometimes violent, game with more contact on the players than on the ball. There were plenty of passes, but very strong ones at that, which often resulted in the ball being taken by the other team, who were vigilant, attentive and always under their feet, making the most of the Swiss team's every slightest error and indecisive moment.'*

The West Auckland miners were a tough bunch and were not going to be intimidated, it only took another two minutes before the ball was again in the Swiss net courtesy of Jock Jones. A shocked Winterthur had no time to relax.

After another round of vigorous handshaking, the West Auckland team continually pressed hard on the Swiss half of the pitch. Arbenz, the Swiss goalkeeper was called into frequent use, as the English threatened to add more goals to their tally. After the half-time break, the teams returned. This time the Swiss were a far livelier team and pushed hard into the English half of the pitch. However, they never really threatened the goal. The English defenders were strong and Tommy Gill in particular, used his head and dribbling skills to clear the lines. Despite the fact that no more goals were scored, the match was a great advert for football. The English team in particular showed great skill with both head and feet. The Swiss were violent in their tackles, but the English players were too smart and avoided many clashes with skill. Their passing was quick and simple. The ball was never held for long and every time the Swiss played a loose ball the English lads took advantage. It was a powerful display of good English football and the watching crowd were lavish in their applause and praise as were the commentators:

'With short, incredibly quick passes, which were almost all done whilst running, without ever stopping the ball, and with some taking advantage of heading the ball, the Black and Whites of West Auckland played a real, classic English game. They often descended on the opposition's goal, but they just couldn't get a shot in. Their style favours precision rather than powerful kicks. They study the keeper's position and knock the ball to where he cannot stop it.'

The West Auckland team were described as superior, skilful, shrewd, united and disciplined. Our romantic Italian reporter was again ready with his pen:

'Then, while the match was coming to an end, the spectators were amazed by the flexible play

of the English team. They admired those players who, wearing their striped shirts filled by the wind, quickly took the ball to the opposing goal. They always attacked in a strong, but not violent way. It was whilst watching this match that football became almost a work of art for me, and I understood the enthusiasm of the English spectators.'

The West Auckland players indeed left the field as winners, with heads held high having achieved what was never thought possible - they had won the Sir Thomas Lipton Trophy, the first true English victory for a World Cup Trophy!

THE AWARD CEREMONY

It was just around 7 p.m. as the match finished the organising committee ascended the special podium.

The two trainers of the Italian team were called and received a gold medal for their part in preparing the Italian team. Them Mr Godley the English referee was given a gold pen for his services and congratulated on the magnificent way he had handled the tournament. He was called calm, energetic and confident, an expert in the game and the best referee in the whole of Italy. No one, including players, had anything to complain of in any match of the tournament.

The German team, Stuttgart were then called forward as the forth (and last) placed team. Each of the team was given a souvenir medal of the occasion. The mixed Italian team were announced as holders of third place, each received their silver souvenir medal. The Swiss team Winterthur went forward to receive their runner-up prizes. They were given the Count Leonino da Zara's magnificent silver plate and each member was given a large silver medal. Finally, the West Auckland team came forward to great applause to receive the amazing Sir Thomas Lipton Trophy. Bob Jones stepped forward to receive the Turin Municipality Gold Cup and a magnificent gold pencil case from Dr Ravi Svorni. Then each member of the team was given a specially engraved silver medal.

These men from West Auckland, who had stepped up to the plate to carry the flag of England to Italy, had acquitted themselves marvellously. They had shown courage against physically tough competition. They had endured strong violent tackles and never once retaliated. They allowed their prowess as footballers to speak for them. Their style of play and skill had impressed all who saw them. As our seasoned Italian reporter wrote their play 'was a work of art'. They were a tribute to their country and to their tiny village nestling in the valley of south Durham.

On the Tuesday following the Tournament the victorious West Auckland side played a further friendly against the Italian team. The Italian team spent the first half throwing everything at the English team, hoping to prove a point, following their showing in the Tournament. It was in the second half that West Auckland pushed hard on the Italian goal and scored a great goal. However, it only encouraged the Italians even more and just before the final whistle they managed to grab an equaliser following a penalty award. The match ended in a draw and was described as a 'brilliant' match. It is interesting that Juventus wanted to play the 1909 team. However, the Italian organisers were adamant it would not happen. They released a statement:

> *'Contrary to what was published yesterday in a local newspaper West Auckland F.C. will not be able to play against the Juventus team next Friday, nor with any other team from Turin, due to*

explicit conditions fixed by mutual agreement between the Organising Committee of the Second Tournament and West Auckland F.C.'

In light of what would happen in 1911, one wonders what a meeting now would have brought about?

The first of the three pre-arranged matches with Vercelli deserves a mention, as it gives insight into how the team were feeling after the Tournament. Unione Sportiva Pro Vercelli, were a major team in Italy, winning the league regularly. Their players were normally the backbone of the Italian national side. They were a team known for their hard tackling. The reports of the match, which was drawn, give an impression of a team who treated the West Auckland lads with respect. One hundred members of the club turned up at the station to greet the team. Mr Godley the referee from the Tournament travelled with them to take charge of the game (He was given an engraved silver referee's whistle). The team arrived at midday and were taken to the fabulous Vercelli gym, to be honoured and toasted by the good and the great of the town. Syd Barron led the team onto the pitch and the Italian band of the 53rd infantry regiment played a magnificent rendering of the English National Anthem. Two thousand people turned out to watch the match, which for a mid-week match was considered excellent. The West Auckland team were described as tired, bruised and with legs bandaged. This was attributed to their gruelling match with the Swiss and the Germans. Their willingness to turn out for the match was a tribute to their courage and desire to honour their commitments.

The West Auckland men travelled to Milan for another friendly. What is interesting here is that they arrived in Milan and Cook's Tours had fouled up the booking. In an interview with Lloyd Thomas, son of Ticer Thomas, he recalled his father telling him they arrived at eleven o'clock at night and a policeman found them on the main street. They explained the situation and they were advised that the best place to sleep would be on the steps of the cathedral. This was due to the policeman telling them that they would be exposed to gangs of thieves. However, because of religion, the muggers never went near the cathedral! So, on that warm night they settled down on the cathedral steps ready to meet Milan the next day. Lloyd's dad Ticer also recalled that for playing at Milan, with such a huge crowd, the team was given their gate share in Lira. Apparently, it was given to Syd Barron in a leather bag that 'Syd kept guarded better than any soldier!' Syd would later change the Lira in Paris and bought the team a very generous supply of beer.

It was now time that the conquering heroes returned to their home village and where they did get a well-deserved enthusiastic reception. They were paraded around the village minus their trophy, which remained in France. The reports were that they were drunk and forgot it. Lloyd was able to give his dad's story of what happened. There was a problem with the customs who were asking for duty on the trophy. However, the team were so full of the beer from Syd they forgot to go to the customs and redeem the trophy. This was later resolved and the trophy was duly sent to West Auckland. However, nothing was reported in the local press of any great import. It is hard to overstate the achievement of the West Auckland Team. They had been playing around the Durham area in the various leagues. They always gave an honest account of themselves and despite their financial struggles held the team together. They were hard working miners who had pride, courage and great personal resources. They took the challenge of a very long journey in those days and took on the best that Italy, Germany and Switzerland could muster and they triumphed. The only report that can be found of the great triumph of these miners was a report in the Newcastle Chronicle, that amounted to no more than a few lines! The 1911 squad, as we will see, got better acknowledgement before and after, but their success, great as it was, would not have been possible if the 1909 lads had not done the business first.

THE MINERS' TRIUMPH

Thomas Lipton's Parents

A Greek figure playing with a football

Calcio being played in an Italian Square

Richard Mulcaster

Copa de Caridad Lipton

> ★ ★ ★
> West Auckland and Eldon sports were not very exciting but purely local in interest. At West Auckland it is to be regretted that the club does not get more financial help from the better-to-do residents. They are a decent bunch of fellows connected with the Football Club, and they should get a bit more patronage from their swell citizens

The Northern Echo report on the financial need of the club

The 1909 Tournament is announced

La squadra inglese.

La squadra inglese impegnata nel nostro Torneo si annuncia sotto ogni rapporto formidabile.

Il *West Auckland F. B. C.*, che fa parte della più importante Federazione di Amateurs del Nord Inghilterra, ha annunciato di voler intervenire coi suoi migliori elementi, e date le brillanti vittorie da essa riportate su Clubs di fama mondiale, i suoi *exploits* in Italia non mancheranno di riuscire un'ottima lezione di gioco per i nostri appassionati *foot-ballers*.

Fra le numerose vittorie riportate dai nostri futuri ospiti in questa stagione citeremo solo a titolo di onore quella avuta sul *Northern Nomads*, il Club che, entrato in finale per la « Coppa di Manchester » contro il *Manchester City F. B. C.* (uno dei più forti *teams* professionisti inglesi), riuscì a sostenere ben quattro *matches* prima di venir battuto 1-0.

Il *South-Bank F. B. C.*, che viene considerato come il Club Amateur più forte d'Inghilterra, è stato pur esso battuto dal *W. A. F. B.* 4-2 in un *match* di campionato, due settimane addietro.

Gli allenamenti razionali ai quali si sottopongono gli atleti d'oltre Manica quando s'impegnano in una competizione internazionale dell'importanza del nostro Torneo, ci fanno prevedere la forma perfetta in cui si presenterà la squadra che giungerà a difendere i colori dell'Inghilterra.

L'intervento di questo sceltissimo gruppo di campioni della verde Albione, senza precedenti in Italia, segnerà certamente una delle più belle pagine del *foot-ball* italiano.

The Italian report confirming the West Auckland team

Grand Order of the Crown of Italy and the Order of St. Sava Medal

STOCKTON v WEST AUCKLAND.

The above friendly fixture took place on the Victoria Ground, Stockton, on Saturday. The weather was fine, but cold, and there was only a poor company of spectators present. Stockton won the toss and elected to play with the sun in their favour. Auckland started and made a brief excursion into the home territory, but hands being given against them, they were quickly driven back. Smart play by Stockton resulted in the leather being put over. The ball was returned, but Dermont getting possession quickly changed the venue of play, but he failed to score, the ball going into bye. The visitors then assumed the aggressive but were unlucky, two shots just going over the bar. The Stocktonians relieved the pressure and good combination among the forwards gave Daniels a chance to score and this he did with a clever shot. Dermont, Stockton's right outside, made several good runs, but was unfortunate in shooting. For a while the homesters had the best of the play, which was, however, of only an uninteresting character. Cochrane took a shot from mid-field, but the globe went wide. A strong pressure was placed upon the visitors' defence, and several strong onslaughts were made, but the visitors' backs displaying good judgment and the Stockton forwards poor shooting, the result was no further score was made. Eventually from a good centre Marquand shot, but the ball struck the post, and on the rebound Hutchinson got possession and notched Stockton's second goal. Shortly after Cochrane centred, and Marquand made amends for his previous disappointment by adding a third with a clinking shot. Stockton continued to show better form than the visitors, and Hutchinson very nearly again put through. Auckland had a look in, and Hird put over the cross-bar. The home men then attacked, and through the instrumentality of Marquand, who put in a fine centre, Daniels cleverly added another, the fourth to Stockton's total. No further score was made up to half-time. Half-time score: Stockton, 4 goals; West Auckland, nil. On crossing over the play was quickly forced by Stockton, and two corners were obtained with no result. After being hemmed in for a considerable time the Aucklandites got down, and made Taylor handle, but the ball was returned. The visitors made another attempt to score by means of Hind, who made a good run on the left and concluded by shooting, but the ball went over. Stockton replied well, but Dermont mulled. For a long time the visitors were unable to get over the centre line, but at last they made a feeble attempt to score, but Taylor easily saved. The remainder of the game was entirely in favour of Stockton. Dermont out of a scrimmage got the fifth goal for Stockton, and the same player within a brief interval scored another. Final result:—Stockton, six goals; West Auckland, nil. Teams:—

Stockton:—Goal, Taylor; backs, J Boyd and E Worden; half-backs, W Monteith (capt.), J Cochrane, T Robson; forwards, J Dermont, J Fairburn, R Daniels, G Hutchinson, and P Marquand.

West Auckland:—Goal, W Howe; backs, W Moore, and H Watson; half-backs, G Smith, J W Boddy, J Davison; forwards, E B Lamb, A Wilkinson, W Salkeld, W Maskell, and H Hird.

The report of the Stockton v West Auckland game 1893

Martin Connolly

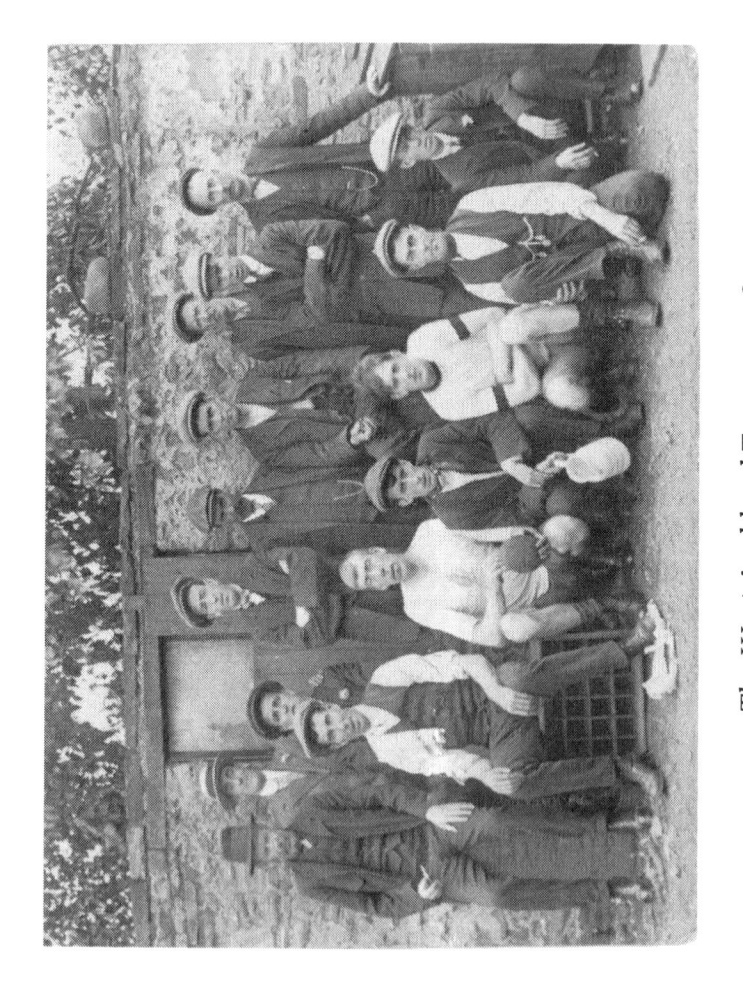

The West Auckland Team c.1908

SIR T. LIPTON AND AN AUCKLAND LADY.

Previous to the yacht races between Shamrock III. and Reliance, Miss Ethel N. Ion, of Bishop, Auckland, executed a pen and ink sketch of the English challenger, with her skipper, Capt. Robt. Wringe, and forwarded it to Sir Thomas Lipton, together with a letter hoping for the success of Shamrock. It is evident that Sir Thomas has been highly pleased with the drawing, which he has acknowledged in the following letter, enclosing a beautifully designed badge, representing his yacht's racing flag:—

        S.Y. Erin, Sandy Hook, N.Y.,
               Aug. 24th, 1903.

Dear Miss Ion,—I duly received your letter, as also the excellent picture, which I am very pleased to have, and which I much appreciate. Please accept my warmest thanks for your kindness, and also the enclosed badge which represents Shamrock's racing flag, and which I hope you will accept with my best wishes.—Yours faithfully,
             THOMAS LIPTON.

Ethel Ion and Lipton's letter

Mr Godley, The Englishman announced as referee

Martin Connolly

Tommy Gill and Eldon Albion with one of their many trophies

THE MINERS' TRIUMPH

The newspaper reveals the trophy for the competition

Martin Connolly

The Teams who would compete in the tournament. West Auckland are on the left of the picture

THE MINERS' TRIUMPH

The four captains

The Four goalkeepers

Martin Connolly

The West Auckland team get the front-page treatment

THE MINERS' TRIUMPH

Turin's Porta Nuova station

Team captain Rob Jones

John (Jack) Greenwell

La squadra italiana che diede una brillante dimostrazione dei grandi progressi dei nostri foot-b
(Fot. Ambrosio e C.

The Italian team

The Swiss 1909 team

THE MINERS' TRIUMPH

Italian and Swiss team take the field 1909

z
The Italian Faroppa, beaten by the swiss Lang in the 1909 match

Martin Connolly

The West Auckland team relax at the 1909 Tournament to watch the Italian v Swiss game

THE MINERS' TRIUMPH

The victorious 1909 West Auckland team

Martin Connolly

The English team challenge the German forwards

belli ricorda con compiacenza d'esser stato portato in trionfo a Genova, dopo due epici *matches* vittorio-   anni Giuocò sempre nel S. Gallo, occupando il posto di *forward*. Venuto l'anno scorso a Torino, Bollinger

La squadra tedesca del Fusbal-Verein Stuttgarter Sportfreunde che parteciperà al nostro 3° Torneo.

The Italian report on the Stuttgart team

110

THE MINERS' TRIUMPH

The 1909 Tournament medal

The Sir Thomas Lipton Trophy

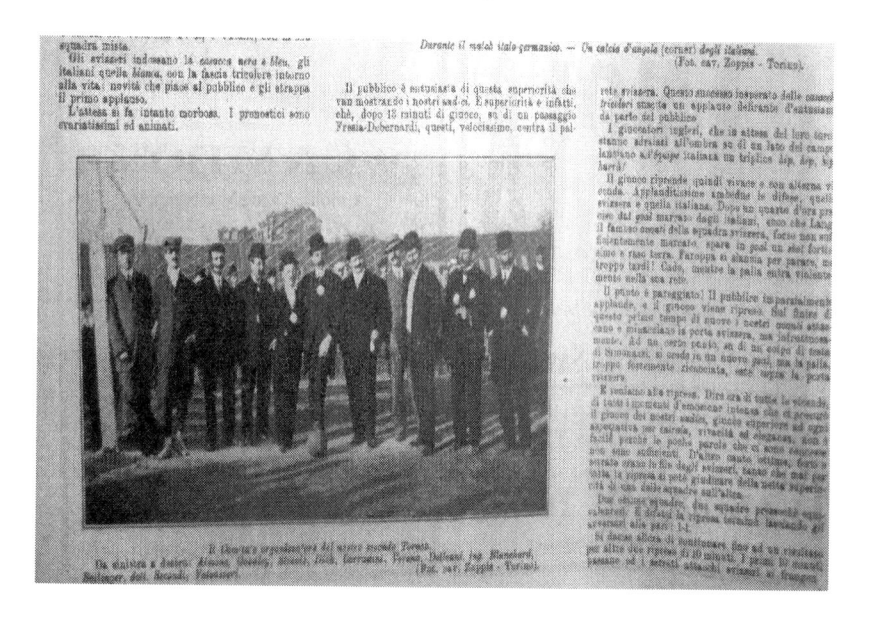

The report of the Italian organisers who put together a great Tournament and laid on a wonderful spread for the Victorious West Auckland Squad representing England

THE MINERS' TRIUMPH

"Newcastle Chronicle"
13-9-09

PLAY AND PLEASURE.

The present day footballer manages to season his sport with a fair amount of pleasure. A correspondent tells me that there are at least two northern amateur clubs which can rival the professional organisations in sharing the tit-bits of enjoyment. These clubs are those of West Auckland and Bishop Auckland. Last season both of the clubs inaugurated Continental tours, West Auckland making a journey to Italy and Bishop Auckland to Belgium. Bishop Auckland won an international amateur trophy at Brussels, and West Auckland became the first holders of the Sir Thos. Lipton Challenge Cup offered for international competition at Turin. As holders of these trophies both clubs aspire for their possession another season, and should everything fare well with them, the committees of each are intent upon sending the players back to the scenes of their past successes. In both instances, however, it is settled that if the tours are again undertaken they will be extended over a larger area. The officials of the Bishop Auckland Club aim at a day or two in Paris after the players fulfil their football engagements at Brussels, whilst West Auckland supporters of the winter pastime have outlined a very ambitious programme, the present intention being not only to pay a return visit to Turin, Genoa, and Vechelli, but also to cross the northern district of Italy to Venice.

The Newcastle Chronicle report of the 1909 Tournament win by West Auckland

THE 1911 TOURNAMENT

The West Auckland team returned from Italy to their routine of work and local amateur football. The 1908/9 season had seen them 10th in the league with an improvement in the 1909/10 season to 5th. This was also the team's position in 1910/11 – their last season before they quit the league.

Due to internal issues in Italy, no Tournament was held in 1910. On the 7th March 1911 the Italian Football Federation approved the Tournament that would involve Juventus, Torino, Zurich F C and West Auckland Football Club, the trophy holders. It was scheduled to take place on the 16th and 17th April. Despite the 1909 visit, the Italian organisers were still confusing another club's record with West Auckland. The facts they give of the expected 1911 team are again very close to those of Bishop Auckland.

'This year the English team West Auckland F.C., the same team that won the first prize in our tournament three years ago (the luxurious challenge of Sir Lipton) will return among us to defend possession of the coveted prize, such as the tournament rules demand. Now the English team has become one of the most talented in Britain, a lot more skilled that the last time they came to Italy. In fact, this year the team has players on its side from the team that won the England "amateurs" Cup, the great Durham Cup, the Northern Championship and so on.'

The truth was that in 1909/10 RMLI Gosport, had won the Amateur Cup at the Bishop Auckland ground and in 1910/11 Bishop Auckland had been runners-up. As to the Durham Cup, Bishop Auckland had last won it in 1899 but they did win the Northern League in 1908/09 and 1910/11. At this point in their history West Auckland had never any success in any of these competitions, although they did have success in the Mid-Durham League before they joined the Northern League.

However, this time they had names of the players in advance. Charlie Parker Hogg, Bob Guthrie and Bob Jones would return from the 1909 squad. Joining them would be John Warwick, a 25-year-old, born at Middle Rainton Sunderland, County Durham), was unmarried and lived in Bishop Auckland. He was a miner who joined the Army. He was a passionate player and would turn out for other teams as well as West Auckland. Michael Alderson was a 27-year-old single lad born in St Helens Auckland and lived in West Auckland. He was a fitter at the local pit. Andy Appleby was 26 and was a hewer at the pit. Born in Shildon, he lived at St Helens Auckland. He was married to Margaret and had no children when he set off to Turin. Not much is known about Charlie Cassidy who went with the team. It is likely that he was a single lad of 25 and worked as a general labourer at the pit. He lived at Witton Park, near West Auckland.

James Robinson was a 28-year-old born in West Auckland, married to Emma with two children, they lived in Bishop Auckland. He was a hewer at the pit. Thomas Riley was a 26-year-old who was a labourer at the local pit (A job that required a lot of stamina). He was a single lad who was born in West Auckland and lived at Toadpool, West Auckland. Bob Moore, was 28 years of age, born in Stanley and lived at West Auckland. He was married to Jane and had five children. He worked at the local pit as a hewer. Fred Dunn, born in Shildon, was 28 and a weighman at the pit. He was married to Alice and had two children. The family lived with Fred's Father and Mother at Shildon. Joe Rewcastle, born in West Auckland, was a 27-year-old hewer at the local pit. Married to Elizabeth he had one daughter and lived in West Auckland. John Thomas Wilson was a 27-year-old hewer, married to Sarah Ann. He was born at Etherley and lived at Cockfield. The Italian organisers also had three other players named in the squad. One was Albert Gill who was a younger brother of the Gill lads who were part of the 1909 Squad. He lived at West Auckland and worked as a hewer at the local pit. He was 23, married to Catherine with one daughter. George Summerson Parker was a 26-year-old miner, married to Edith and they lived at the Blacksmith Arms at Spring Gardens, which was owned by Edith's mother, who was a widow. William Holmes was a 20-year-old, born in West Auckland and living at St Helens Auckland. He was single and worked as a Coke Cooler at the pit. It is not clear if they actually made the trip, but it is thought they may have gone as substitutes. The report of how the matches would be played was announced:

> 'During the last meeting the Committee decided the matches by drawing the names out of a box. On the first day (April 18th) the matches will take place on the Juventus pitch and on Torino F.C.'s pitch on the second day. The first match will be Juventus against Zurich F.C. and the second one will be Torino F.C. against the English team. The winners will then measure up against each other for first and second place, and the losers will

compete for third and fourth place. In addition to the Lipton Cup, other prizes will be awarded. There will be a prize of the king and the Municipality. Moreover, the baron Leonino da Zara offered a beautiful silver plaque and Turin's company "Megard" offered another valuable artistic trophy. La Stampa Sportiva will give to the captain of each team a big silver medal.'

The club officials, Miles Barron along with Eddie Meek (a foreman at the pit), Ralph Hodgson (a hewer), and Bob Chamberlain (a building contractor) would accompany the team. Again, the financial burden placed on the team was tremendous. The truth was that the players had very little resources and very few possessions they could sell to raise funds. But with a combination of what they could sell and donations (and indeed borrowing), the team was able to make the journey once again. This time they were sent on their way to the sound of a brass band and they left West Auckland on the Wednesday 12th April. The journey would take them to London where the boat train carried them to Dover and then over the channel to Calais and onward by train to Turin. All the way there was the banter and sing-song like any other travelling team. After a stop at Abbeville for lunch they travelled on to reach Paris at 11p.m. Despite the long journey the lads had a quick wash and refresh and headed into Paris, which most of the team had never seen before and were totally enthralled by the boulevards and buildings they saw. The following day was spent sight-seeing and this included a boat trip on the Seine. They then made their way through Switzerland, once again mesmerised by the scenery, especially the awesome sight of Mont Blanc.

The Simplon, a twelve and a half mile long, tunnel took them through to the Italian country side. Here Syd recalls the sight of men and women labouring in the fields. Eventually they arrived in Turin and the anticipation of football took over the excitement of being tourists and the focus was now on making sure they would repeat the success of the 1909 team.

THE MINERS' TRIUMPH

FIRST DAY OF THE 1911 TOURNAMENT

The first match was between Juventus and Zurich on the 16th April. The match would be refereed by Syd Barron. It was widely expected that Zurich would easily win the game. They had come to the tournament with an unbeaten record and hailed as one of the great teams of Europe. The match was a pretty mediocre affair. Juventus were in the middle of a bad club dispute, in which Juventus as a team had many divisions. The club's management were in the throes of a possible dissolution of the team over performance and money. It was thought this would affect the players. The Juventus team never played with any great flair. It is true that their forwards pressed on the Zurich goal and that the defence held the Swiss reasonably well. However, this was more to do with the Swiss not really ever getting into their stride that had them at the top of the Swiss League. The result of

2-0 for Juventus was a great surprise to all, even the Italians. The only notable player on the pitch was Pannano, the Juventus keeper, who kept a clean sheet. Even with their win Juventus were described as not operating as a unified team, having no preciseness or decisiveness in their play. At the end of the day, Juventus coming through this opening match has to be laid at the door of a very under-performing Swiss side. The Italian report was direct:

> 'The Zurich team on the other hand did not live up to our expectations, despite having a very promising team that was organised in defence and outstanding in attack. How then were they beaten by Juventus? This result certainly shocked a few people, especially considering that Zurich are near the top of the Swiss League whilst Juventus are near the bottom of the Italian League.'

The second match to take place was West Auckland against Torino. This was a far better match. Torino did not come to the game to be spectators. They immediately set out their ambition by attacking the English goal. They continually played with skill and determination and went ahead in the fifteenth minute. The West Auckland team was knocked back by Torino's unexpected onslaught and were galvanised to tighten up and make reply. They were reported to be strong and courageous, and so it proved as Moore received a beautiful pass that he picked up and with great skill, thumped the ball into Torino's goal.

The second half saw Torino come again to win the match, and they soon had slotted the ball past Warwick to go into the lead. Again, the West Auckland lads were not to be undone and worked hard to push Torino back. It was not long before the West Aucklanders used great dribbling skills to get the ball through the Torino defence and once more equal the score. As one reporter wrote:

'Together, they concentrate all of their efforts on passing the ball around, so fantastically, as if they were all part of one intricate web. This allows them to keep their opponents under constant pressure when attacking and to keep themselves well organised in the defence.'

The matched ebbed and flowed into both teams' halves but finally in the eighty-sixth minute West Auckland managed once more to get the ball into Torino's net. The West Auckland team trooped off the field, having come through a tough match. Whilst the Italians had shown some good class, their game was marred by their rough play. They continually used any attempt by West Auckland to jump for a high ball, to elbow their opponent in the back. In tackles, there was no attempt to simply play the ball, but if an ankle could be tapped hard, it was. The physical nature of the game and the hot weather took its toll on the players, as did the long journey, but the West Auckland Team had made it through and would now play Juventus in the final match to decide the Tournament winners.

SECOND DAY OF THE 1911 TOURNAMENT

Monday, the 17th April 1911 saw the dawn of a great day for West Auckland. The weather was again hot and sticky. The first match of the day was the decider for third place between Zurich and Torino.

This was another match in which both teams did not give a great display. The Italian press gave very little space to the match and in the few comments they made they were not even over-complimentary about their own team, even though they ran out 2-1 winners.

> *'Our centre forwards never seem to move as a solid whole and surprise the rival defence. And they lack decisiveness and precision in shots that, taken*

from a far, catch the goalkeeper unaware and get past his defence.'

By 4.30 in the afternoon, the day had become a little cooler, when Mr Meazza from Milan blew his whistle for the kick-off between West Auckland and Juventus. The press described West Auckland's team as 'balding, clumsy and energetic', as they ran onto the pitch. The sun was on their back and they were notably well refreshed and rested after their match the previous day. The Juventus players looked physically weak and intimidated by the West Auckland miners, hardened by the long hours hewing coal underground. From the very beginning they took control. Their dribbling of the ball and smart passing was artful.

The press again reported them as 'the true masters of the game'. Pannano, described as the best Italian player, was showered with shots in the first three minutes from the West Auckland forwards. It was one of these shots, from Moore, that hammered the back of Pannano's net - the first goal to West Auckland. The Juventus team simply pulled everyone back and the goal was a mass of bodies that was more a hindrance to the goalkeeper, than a help. On the ninth minute another great pass landed on Appleby's head and the goalkeeper stood no chance as it whistled by him.

Two minutes later it was Rewcastle's turn to contribute to the party, and with a cracking shot he made the score 3-0. Juventus were by now reeling and disorganised. It was the fourteenth minute when Dunn took the ball and with great dribbling and strength, passed Juventus' defenders and placed the ball neatly under the flaying arms of Pannano. The crowd were applauding and calling for more goals, but not for Juventus, rather it was for the amazing English miners who were taking Juventus apart. Play went on with West Auckland in full control and Juventus looking for the half-time whistle, which eventually came to allow a fifteen-minute break, in which Juventus hoped to regroup.

The second half got underway and West Auckland came out as if no break had occurred and were immediately at the Juventus defence. With more dribbling and great passes and often using their heading ability, the English team totally dominated. At times it appeared the Juventus players were standing back to watch the West

Auckland team play. Just after five minutes, Moore was again active in the forward line and another goal was chalked up. 5-0. In the tenth minute of the second half, the ball came to Dunn's feet and with great power, a low ground shot skipped over the grass and under the diving body of Pannano, 6-0.

Now the crowd were no longer happy with the Italian team. Boos rang around the ground as it was made clear what the Italian supporters thought of Juventus. This no doubt stirred Juventus, but The West Auckland team were relentless in storming into Juventus' half. They were completely dominating the game and there was no way they were losing this match. However, Juventus summoned up a bit of pride and tried to push up to the West Auckland goal. They managed to get two or three shots on target but couldn't get past Warwick. That was until a corner was awarded to Juventus. The ball came into Corbelli, who jumped high in the air and netted the ball. It was a simple goal that Juventus treated as a major win, celebrating their loss of face with great enthusiasm. However, it was to be their only success of the day.

West Auckland continued to dominate and only the brilliance of Pannano, in Juventus' goal stopped a further five or six goals going in. The relief for Juventus was in the final whistle that brought their suffering to an end, as West Auckland left the field with a tremendous 6-1 win. This win was in itself an amazing feat for a team, mainly miners, from the Northern League in England. Yet it was more than this. The Italian press reports were glowing in their praise of the team. Described as having a passion for the game, they were expert in dribbling the ball. They were sharp and shrewd in their passing ability. They were organised and relied on skill, not violence. They were a tribute to their country. The Italian press once more bemoaned the standard of their country's football and the reality of having been taught a lesson by the miners from West Auckland:

> 'Now we must learn lessons from the higher level! After two years we have already learned two clear lessons. Let's hope we can make the best of them. Italian teams have once again shown their Achilles' heel: the first line in both the Turinese

teams   lacks   cohesion, particularly Juventus.'

The team duly attended the award ceremony where the team captain Michael Alderson received the trophy and thanked the organising committee on behalf of the team. He received his captain's silver medal which was proudly received on behalf of the conquering heroes, who had defended their honour and their country's football reputation. Syd Barron also made a speech complimenting the efficiency of the event and was very sporting in his remarks to the other competitors.

Later a dinner was held at the Swiss Club in Turin, where Carlo Litz, on behalf of the organisers welcomed the dignitaries and teams. The vice-president of Torino, Castoldi and Malvano, the president of Juventus, complimented the winners and praised football as the ultimate winner. Syd Barron was then given the floor, representing the victorious English side. He addressed the gathering in Italian, praising the organisers and thanking them for their hospitality towards the West Auckland team.

The Italian organisers published a photograph which showed among the team, three players, Albert Gill,

Willie Holmes and George Parker. These three were apparently expected to travel to Turin as substitutes, but the documents do not show if they played in any of the matches. Albert was a brother of the Gill lads from 1909 and George would later go on to captain West Auckland in later years. The team would spend the next few days playing three friendlies against Milan (3-1 win), Turin (2-1 win) and Genoa (1-1 draw) before they would make their long journey home. For those who would doubt West Auckland were the first *English* team to win 'the World Cup', it is noticeable that when England played their friendly against Italy in 1933, the official view, published in the press in 1933, was that West Auckland were indeed the first ever national English team that had played Italy and beaten them and won an international trophy. Other English teams followed them including clubs such as Liverpool etc.

Once again, as in 1909, on their way home the customs raised the question of duty for the cup and eventually the matter was resolved with a 'loan' of £40 from the Wheatsheaf Hotel's (the team's local) landlady Mrs Lanchester. The cup followed the team later. The team arrived back to an enthusiastic welcome, celebrating their defence of the trophy and more so as they would now hold it permanently, having won it twice.

Football was not the gold-mine of modern football. The financial burden on the team members and the club itself was crippling. It was therefore decided to pull out of the Northern League. Not only this, they could not afford to pay back the loan and the trophy was now in the ownership of Mrs Lanchester.. In March 1912 the club informed the Northern league it was heavily in debt. The West Auckland Football Club was officially closed.

Martin Connolly

The Italian press photo of the 1911 West Auckland Team

THE MINERS' TRIUMPH

John Warwick defends his goal against Torino in the 1911 Tournament

The Juventus 1911 team

il campo del F. C. Torino. — La seconda giornata del Torneo. Durante il match di consolazione fra il F. C. Zurich e il F. C. Torino. - Un corner sulla porta torinese. (Fot. cav. Zoppis - Torino).

The press captures a corner kick in the Torino v Zurich match in the

Il 3° Torneo Internazionale di Foot-ball a Torino

The Zurich team who took the field in the 1911 Tournament

THE MINERS' TRIUMPH

Another attack on the Juventus goal by West Auckland in the 1911 final

The Swiss score their only goal in the playoff against Torino in 1911

Martin Connolly

The West Auckland Working Men's Club Committee who gave their support to the team

A DIFFERENT KIND OF FIGHT

The West Auckland Football Club was gone but the players still wanted to play and a number of them continued to turn out for other local teams. By 1913 there was a desire to resurrect the club and it again took its place among the amateur teams. They played across different minor leagues in Durham. Under the name St Helens United, the team played for a season in the Northern League in 1919. They again re-joined the Northern League in 1934 as West Auckland Football Club.

In 1911 when the Tournament in Italy was played, no one could have foreseen the terrible events that would engulf Europe. On the 28th July 1914 war broke out. Then it was called the Great War and many of the men of West Auckland, who had fought for a trophy on the football fields at Turin, would now have a very different fight on the many battle fields across Europe. The bombings on London in the Second World War destroyed many of the records of the men who campaigned in the Great War. It is therefore hard to get accurate information on all the players from the 1909 and 1911 tournaments.

William Holmes joined the East Yorkshire Regiment. He served in Alexandria and France and rose to the rank of Lt. Corporal. It was on the battlefield of France that he was
killed in action. The death of this man who died for his country is simply recorded in army records on a faded hand-written notation, indicating he was killed at the very beginning of the conflict.

Andy Appleby joined the Durham Light Infantry and served in France. His record shows him as a driver and mechanic. He appears to have been caught up in one of the many gas attacks and even though he served for most of the war, he was troubled with various bouts of illness, He was transferred to Nottingham where he served as a labourer. He was discharged in September 1918 having done his duty to the country.

John Warwick, West Auckland's goalkeeper, also served with the Durham Light Infantry. In the valley of the river Aisne, one of the toughest confrontations with the Germans took place. The Germans initially on the higher ground pummelled the British advance. It was during such a battle that John acted with great bravery. His commanding officer wrote to Head Quarters recommending him for a VC, as recorded in the local press.

The response was not to award the VC but he was awarded the Distinguished Conduct Medal. His citation notes his actions. He also rose from Private to Corporal. Throughout the war and after John continued to play his football, turning out regularly for South Shields.

The war records of other members of the team could not be found, but these three records demonstrate the courage and commitment of the men who not only faced the dangers of the enemy at war, but who in peace time met their opponents on the football field and triumphed.

Robert Chamberlain, the club's treasurer, served with the Royal Engineers. He served in Europe and

Mesopotamia and saw out the war, giving six years of service. After the war he gave up being a building contractor, building houses and went to work in Middlesbrough.

AND THE REST....

The passage of time obscures many of the details of what happened to the various members of the two teams. However, there are some who have left their mark, as well as those above who served in the Great War.

John (Jack) Greenwell was a great local player for Crook F C and had often turned out for West Auckland when they were short of a player.

He won many honours with Crook and there was no doubting his footballing talent. His trip abroad must have stirred something in him as in 1912 he moved to live in Spain. With football in his blood Jack soon joined the Barcelona team and played eighty-eight matches for them. He was a part of a winning side and eventually he took on the role of manager at the club. He was one of their most successful managers. After Barcelona, he also managed Mallorca, Valencia and Sporting de Gijon. His management work was also international, when he helped the Peru team to success. He had a time in Turkey and finally in Columbia where he worked with their emerging team. This great man of football ended his days in Columba, where he died of a heart attack in 1942.

Tommy Gill returned and continued to play his local football with West Auckland and Eldon Albion. He decided not to join the 1911 trip due to the expense and he felt happy that he had already had an achievement that could not be bettered. His descendants still live in the area and have fond memories of him. He was a hardworking and well-liked man, who remained in mining until he finally retired. He had one habit they remember well which was that he had to have a daily pint down at his local! Indeed, on visiting the local pubs in West Auckland many residents were always ready to stand Tommy a pint. Tommy was proud of his part in the Sir Thomas Lipton trophy and always wore his medal on a watch chain. Jeannie Franklin's family, who inherited Tommy's medal, have given it as a long-term loan to the National Football Museum in Manchester, where it can be seen on display.

David Ticer Thomas was born in Staffordshire and before moving to West Auckland, worked in the pottery industry as a painter of pottery. He was one of the 1909 team who was approached after the Tournament to become a coach in Italy. Mary Ethel his wife would not hear of it. Lloyd Thomas, Ticer's son, laughed as he recalled his father's account of her reaction. I caught up with Lloyd and his son David at Lloyd's home in West Auckland, where he had lived for ninety-four years. Despite his long age Lloyd was still sharp in his memories and was able to recall clearly his father's accounts of his football experiences. The name 'Ticer', Lloyd explained, came from the footballer's ability in cricket. Ticer played for Bishop Auckland cricket club during the summer, when he was not playing for West Auckland at football.

He was a spin bowler and used to entice batsmen to make shots that his terrific ability to spin would catch out. He was the 'Enticer' which was shortened to 'Ticer' and this stuck with him. He explained that his dad came home from Italy and decided to become a referee. He qualified and took charge of many games in the area. As a miner Ticer was in a reserved occupation and at his age he was not called up to service in the Great War. However, he contributed to the war effort, like many other miners, in making sure the coal was available for the nation. An interesting activity Ticer became connected with, was a ladies team in West Auckland with Anne Hogg being the centre forward. Ticer was their coach and manager. Lloyd recalled the team played another ladies team from York. Research has shown that the York ladies were from the Terry's Chocolate Factory Ladies Team. They also came to play Darlington in 1936. Lloyd recalled that a French lady played for the York team and once again his memory was spot on as a Ladies French Team had come from Paris and were playing friendly matches across England. No doubt one was roped in for the match at West Auckland.

The ladies were not allowed to use the official West Auckland Club ground as they were not an FA affiliated team. There was great opposition to ladies football by the FA and referees were eventually banned from assisting them as coach or managers. Ticer demonstrates again the same spirit that took him to the 1909 Tournament in taking on tasks that others would think better off. The photo here shows the Ladies Team which had among its members three of Charlie Parker Hogg's family and he is also seen in the photo, beside Ticer Thomas. Others known to be in the photo are among back row, Wade, N Simpson, Plews, Wade, E Parrish, A Hogg, Monk, in middle row, Meads, E Bannister, M Hogg, Hogg, G Stott, M Hogg, and in front row, H Race, E Marshall, Mr Gill, C Hogg and A Hogg.

Ticer passed his football genes down the family line and his son Lloyd was a goalkeeper and played with Shildon Railway A F C. He was part of the squad that had great success. Lloyd is very proud of his cups and two sit on his sideboard. Lloyd always had a conflict with his football and his love of playing in the brass band. Lloyd saw service in the Royal Engineers during World War Two. The football genes also passed down to Ticer's grandson David who also became known as Ticer. David had fond memories of his World Cup grandfather who would take his grandson onto the football field at the rear of the house. It was there that he passed onto young David the skills that had served him well in Italy. By seven years of age, his grandson was playing for his school team in St Helens Auckland. From here he played as a junior and eventually played for the England Schoolboys Squad. He did not play in the world cup squad in 1966, being only a schoolboy, but he did score a winning goal for England at

Wembley in 1966 against West Germany – in the International Schoolboy competition!

David also played for Burnley at 16 and moved to Queens Park Rangers. In his career he played for Everton, Wolves, Vancouver Whitecaps, Middlesbrough and Portsmouth. David played eight times for the senior England squad as a right winger. At the end of his playing career David entered the teaching profession as a P E Teacher, now retired he lives in Barnard Castle. He and his brother kept a keen eye on their parents, Lloyd and Jessie in their West Auckland home until unfortunately Lloyd sadly passed away in 2014. The great Dave Ticer Thomas who played his part in the Sir Thomas Lipton 1909 squad would have been immensely proud of his son and grandson who pulled on an England shirt and carried on the family's proud tradition of International footballing heroes.

As we noted earlier, Captain Bob Jones was born Robert Ovington, and apparently used the name Jones. He originally played for Bishop Auckland but felt out of place among the professional classes that included solicitors, who played for them. Bob's younger brother George speaking in 1985 said Bob was offered a job in Italy as a trainer but his wife Edith refused to go not wanting to have to eat the foreign food, such as 'frog legs'. And so it was that Bob returned to West Auckland Football Club and continued to turn out for them when he came back from Italy. He eventually returned to using Ovington as his name and lived to the ripe old age of 92. Whenever West played at home Bob would be there. He died after a fall in a Barnard Castle nursing home and after his cremation, his ashes were scattered on the West Auckland Football Club's pitch at the Seaview ground, as he had requested before his death.

Tommy 'Tot' Riley went to the tournament with his brother James (Jack) to support him. The Riley family had lost their mother at a very early age. The boys had been raised by their aunt Elizabeth Bayles (nee Riley). It appears that Tot took on the name Bayles and, on his return, concentrated more on his love of Foot Racing than football. One of Tot's descendants, Neale Vickers, still living in the area, continues to turn out to see West Auckland play every week. He has some postcards that were sent from Italy during the Tournament. They give a flavour of the excitement of the West Auckland miners on that great trip. One card from Tot simply says, '...*enjoying ourselves a treat...*'.

In another he expresses being well and '*about a stone heavier*'. In the same card the goalkeeper John Warwick sends his regards. However, one of the most understated cards that Tot's brother Jack sent simply states,

> '*Dear Father and Mother, Just a line we won the cup yesterday 6-1. Hope you are all keeping well, your loving son,*
> *Jack*'

With such a modest statement the great 6-1 victory over Juventus in 1911 is announced to the village!

A CHAMPION TRIBUTE

In 2008 Rob Yorke, a local councillor, and Friends of West Auckland, decided a memorial should be erected in the village to commemorate the achievement of the World Cup heroes. The idea was brought to the attention of The Parish Council, The Arts Council and private sector companies to raise the necessary funds, estimated at around £185,000. Durham County Council agreed that a statue could be placed on the Village Green. It would not only commemorate the great football story but would also honour the mining history of the village. Both had been combined in the winning of the Sir Thomas Lipton Trophy's story. It would be a bronze statue and would be sculptured by a London-based artist, Nigel Boonham.

It was on a very wet Saturday in October 2013 and the rain was drizzling down, when I caught up with Nigel at the unveiling of the statue. He recalled that when he was given the brief for it, he wanted to make it ambiguous, so that the viewer could have his or her own experience of what they saw. That, Nigel thought, would be different, depending on the viewing angle you approached it from. He created a figure of a miner on the ground, chipping out coal, but that would also be the action of a goalkeeper diving for a ball. He was also keen to emphasise that the height of the standing figure's raised leg, a footballer kicking a ball, was exactly the height of a seam in which a miner worked. Standing with his young daughter looking at the statue, he had a real pride that he had done the West Auckland footballers and miners proud. Few would disagree.

It was also a tribute to the hard work of the local councillors and Football Club officials, who had made the day possible. They deserve great credit. They had invited Tim Healey along to help with the day. He was the actor who played Charlie Hogg in The Captain's Tale. He expressed his delight in being able to be there, noting it was great to see the working miners who had done the seemingly impossible, honoured. Sir John Hall, the former owner of Newcastle United was also there to assist at the event. He too was pleased to see the memorial to a great sporting achievement being given pride of place at the centre of the village. '*It is hard to overstate the magnificence of the miner's achievement and it is right that the community celebrate their victory*', he told me.

It was also an honour to have David Thomas, the grandson of Ticer Thomas of the 1909 squad there. It was thought that the standing figure on the statue was modelled on an image of his grandfather. As we chatted at the unveiling he remarked, '*I am so proud of my grandfather and it is grand to see the memorial at the centre of the village*'. Despite the rain and the wind, the village turned out in good numbers, to acknowledge the honour that their football team had brought to the village.

THE CONTINUING STORY...

West Auckland Football Club remains an active ambitious team. In domestic football they have added to their pre-World Cup successes, such as winning the Mid Durham League in 1905/6. The 1959 season saw them in the first round of the FA Cup proper and winners of the Northern League Division 1 in 1959/60 and 1960/61. 1963 saw them win the Northern League Cup and the Durham Challenge Cup in 1964. In the same season they were FA Amateur Cup runners up and the winners of the Durham Benevolent Bowl.

When they played in Division 2 of the league, they won it in 1990/91 and were runners up in 1997/98. In 1999 they again went to the first round of the FA Cup proper and their runs in the League Cup have also been credible with wins in 1958/59 and 1962/63. They were also runners up in 1948/49, 1961/62, 1963/64 and 2011/12.

The also had a great run in the FA Vase in 2011/12, finishing as runners up. The 2017/18 season found them still battling away in the Northern League finishing fifth in Division 1. A great club with a great history continues.....

Honours:

- Mid-Durham League – Winners 1905/6
- Sir Thomas Lipton Trophy (World Cup) Winners – 1909, 1911
- Northern League Champions – 1959–60
- Northern League Cup Winners – 1959–60, 1962–63
- Durham Benevolent Bowl Winners – 1960–61, 1962–63
- Durham Challenge Cup Winners –1963–64
- FA Amateur Cup Finalists – 1960–61
- FA Cup 1st Round Proper – 1959, 1961, 1999
- FA Vase Finalists – 2011–12, 2013–14
- Durham Challenge Cup Finalists –2015–16

The proud record of this club has attracted many plaudits over the years and the story of the West Auckland team came to the attention of two of the greatest writers from the North east, Ed Waugh and Trevor Wood. They decided Making a drama out of a trophy. They wrote a play *'My Grandfather Knew Alf Ramsay'*, in the play they retell the story of the miners' great achievement. Sitting in the Memorial Hall, West Auckland, watching the play was an amazing experience of tears, laughter and great joy. The packed hall, mainly from the village, was a testament to the on-going pride of the village of West Auckland. Chatting with Ed confirms his great enthusiasm for all things North East, but also demonstrates how the achievement of the West Auckland miners has struck a chord in many hearts of courage and determination. That it is not just a football story but a story of the human capacity for individuals to rise above their humble circumstances and soar to great heights. When Ed met up with Alex Ferguson, the legendary manager of Manchester United, to show him the cup Sir Alex mused that it was the only cup he had never won.

This is the real heart of the story about a team of miners, who for all intents and purposes were just ordinary men. They were given a challenge to become heroes and they came from the pit and climbed to the top of the world.

The faded note on William Holmes war record

The Distinguished Conduct Medal

8757 Pte. J. WARWICK 2nd Bn.
For gallant conduct on 20th September 1914, at Troyon, valley of the Aisne, when he voluntarily assisted in the rescue of a wounded Officer under a heavy fire. (1.4.15)

Army citation of John Warwick's medal

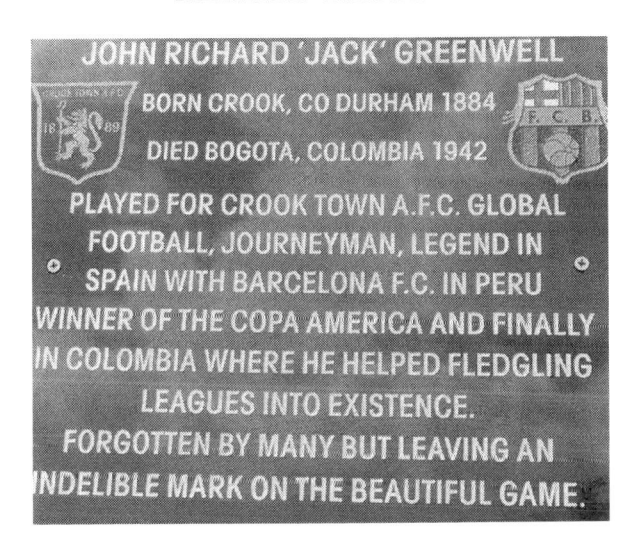

JOHN RICHARD 'JACK' GREENWELL
BORN CROOK, CO DURHAM 1884
DIED BOGOTA, COLOMBIA 1942
PLAYED FOR CROOK TOWN A.F.C. GLOBAL
FOOTBALL, JOURNEYMAN, LEGEND IN
SPAIN WITH BARCELONA F.C. IN PERU
WINNER OF THE COPA AMERICA AND FINALLY
IN COLOMBIA WHERE HE HELPED FLEDGLING
LEAGUES INTO EXISTENCE.
FORGOTTEN BY MANY BUT LEAVING AN
INDELIBLE MARK ON THE BEAUTIFUL GAME.

The plaque, honouring Jock's achievements

Tommy Gill with his daughters, Lily & Maggie. on Tommy's waistcoat is his medal.

> Private J Warwick, who has been recommneded for the Victoria Cross - the first recommendation for this coveted honour during the war - belongs to the 2nd Durham Light Infantry. He is well known in the North as an enthusiastic Association player, and previous to the outbreak of war, he kept goal for West Auckland in the Northern league.

Press report of John Warwick's recommendation for the VC

The grandson of Ticer Thomas with his cap and medals awarded when he played for England

THE MINERS' TRIUMPH

The son and grandson of the 1908 footballing hero, Ticer Thomas: Lloyd and David (Ticer) Thomas

Ticer Thomas' son Lloyd, proudly carries on his dad's cup winning ways with his Shildon AFC, 1937/8 Auckland League Winner's Cup

Lloyd and Jessie Thomas

THE MINERS' TRIUMPH

The West Auckland Ladies Football team with members of the world beating miners' Team

163

Martin Connolly

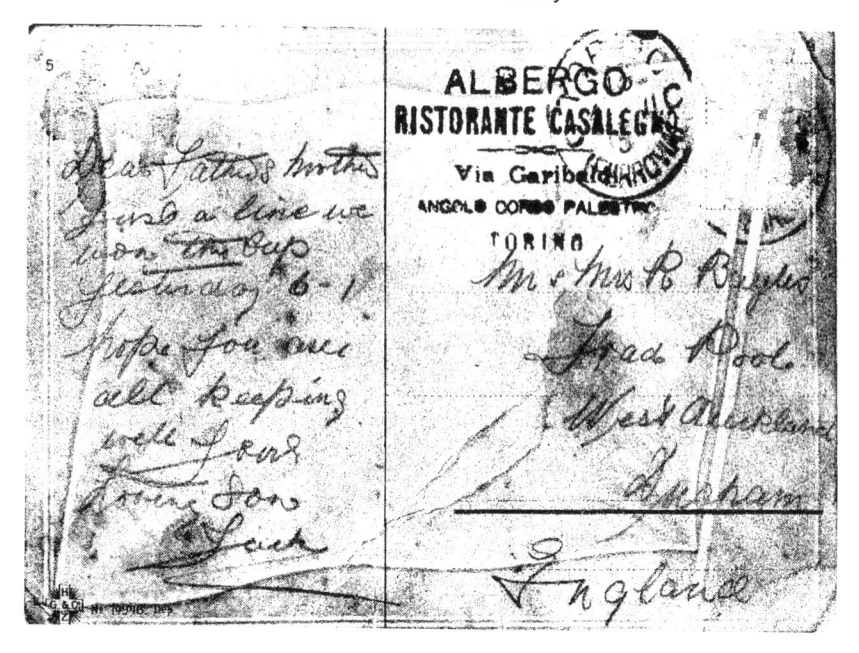

The postcard that announces the win over Juventus – 6 to 1

A post card from Tommy Tot Riley, in Italy, clearly enjoying the food!

THE MINERS' TRIUMPH

The Memorial to the West Auckland Miner's Football teams that stands on the village green opposite the Working Men's Club

Nigel Boonham, the artist who designed the Miner's statue at West Auckland, with his daughter at the unveiling of the memorial statue

Dave (Ticer) Thomas (England footballer and grandson of Ticer Thomas from the 1909 team) along with Tim Healey and Sir John Hall at the unveiling of the memorial

Local Councillors who worked and supported the erection of the memorial, along with Nigel Boonham and Dave Thomas, at the unveiling of the memorial

THE MINERS' TRIUMPH

The West Auckland Football Club's badge, proudly showing the World Football Trophy

Stuart Alderson current General Manager of the club, the, is rightly proud of its history. Here is seen in the clubhouse at the Seagrave ground, which holds many photos and memorabilia from the club's wonderful history.

John Wotherspoon, commercial director of Lipton Teas, said the story of West Auckland FC and their "folk heroes" should never be forgotten.

The unveiling of the memorial statue with the trophy in the foreground

THE MINERS' TRIUMPH

A scene from the play 'My Grandfather Knew Alf Ramsay'

Sir Alex Ferguson and playwright Ed Waugh with the Sir Thomas Lipton trophy

ACKNOWLEDGEMENTS

Writing any book takes a lot of research and the help of others is always necessary. I am therefore grateful to all those who shared their memories and thoughts, as I put this book together, in particular, the following:

The staff at Archivio La Stampa who pointed me to the Italian material.

Donatella Biffignandi of *Museo Nazionale dell'Automobile, Torino*, for letting me freely have his time, taking great trouble to help and allowing me to use the newspapers and photographs from the archives.

Theresa Federici and her students in the Italian Department of Durham University, without whom I could never have understood the Italian documents.

Ticer Thomas' son Lloyd and grandson David for sharing their memories and David for his Foreword.

Jeannie Franklin, for her memories and photographs of Tommy Gill.

Colin Turner of Eldon, a very helpful local historian, especially with anything Eldon.

Ed Waugh for his enthusiasm and permission to use his photographs.

Peter Holme of the National Football Museum for his time and help.

Emma Burgham of the Unilever Archives for her time and useful documents.

Jamie Flett of the Mitchell library, who took time to help my research.

Michael Gallagher, of Glasgow City Archives who pointed me in the right direction for archive material.

The West Auckland Working Men's Club who look after the Trophy and allow photographs to be taken.

Stuart Alderson West Auckland Football Club's General manager (2014) and his trusty volunteers who help out at the ground.

John Wotherspoon, Historian to West Auckland.

Neale Wade a descendent of Tommy Riley for his valued contribution to my research.

...And to the many great people of West Auckland who chatted, argued and laughed with me as we reminisced about the Sir Thomas Lipton Trophy and gave great tales of the wonderful triumph of the West Auckland Miners.

Printed in Poland
by Amazon Fulfillment
Poland Sp. z o.o., Wrocław